Introducing
the Macintosh®

Introducing the Macintosh

Charles Duff

McGraw-Hill Book Company

New York   St. Louis   San Francisco   Auckland   Bogotá
Hamburg   Johannesburg   London   Madrid   Mexico City
Montreal   New Delhi   Panama   Paris   São Paulo
Singapore   Sydney   Tokyo   Toronto

Library of Congress Cataloging in Publication Data

Duff, Charles.
   Introducing the Macintosh.

   (A Byte book)
   Includes index.
   1. Macintosh (Computer) I. Title. II. Series: Byte
books.
   QA76.8.M3D83 1984   001.64   84-9651
   ISBN 0-07-018024-5

Wordstar® is a trademark of Micropro International Corporation. Microsoft® Word, Microsoft® Multiplan,
Microsoft® Chart, Microsoft® File,and MS-DOS® are trademarks of Microsoft Corporation. Microsoft® is a
registered trademark. Apple®, Apple II®, IIe, and III are registered trademarks; and ImageWriter®, Lisa®,
Macintosh®, MacPaint®, and MacWrite® are trademarks of Apple Computer, Inc. XEROX Star® is a registered
trademark of XEROX Corporation. IBM® is a registered trademark. VisiCalc® is a registered trademark of
VisiCorp. Hayes SmartModem® is a trademark of Hayes Microcomputer Products, Inc. CompuServe® is a
registered trademark of CompuServeEL Information Services, Inc. THE SOURCE is a service mark of
Source Telecomputing Corp.

For my Mother and Father

Contents

Preface

This book is intended to serve the needs of two groups of people: those who might be considering the purchase of a personal computer, and those who have already purchased a Macintosh and are looking for additional background on its history, its design and its use.

As a software author with Kriya Systems and member of the initial Macintosh Development Team, I have had an opportunity to work intensively with the Macintosh since well before its release. I became convinced soon after I first experienced the Macintosh that a new era was coming, one which promised to sweep away many of our preconceptions about the process of computing. No longer would the confusion and fear previously experienced by many new users be accepted as an inevitable component of learning to use a computer. One could sit down and in less than an hour expect to profitably use the Macintosh and several of its applications.

This, then would also seem to obviate the need for a host of "how-to" books to fill in the gaps usually left by the manufacturer. In fact, Apple's user manuals are probably the best in the industry, and need little support. What can and should be provided in a book of this type is the larger view, which has the following components:

1. Is the Macintosh truly more useful than other machines, and why?

2. Given that I can learn how to use it more easily, how can it help in my everyday life?

3. What are the new models that the Macintosh uses for human-computer interaction, and why are they better?

4. Where did the new approaches seen in the Macintosh come from, and will they be accepted as a standard? What's next?

This book is not a cookbook or "how-to" manual; to attempt this would be a waste of the author's time and the reader's money. It will enable you to rationally decide whether you should buy a Macintosh and why; it will give detailed background on how and why the Mac was designed, providing any necessary technical background as it proceeds; and it will give you the tools you need to function and make your own decisions in a very sophisticated environment. One of the hidden effects of any progressive technological development such as the Macintosh is a shifting of responsibility from the designer to the user. No longer can we complain about inadequate tools; now we have them and have to actually do something with them, which can be scarier and more threatening than the alternative.

The book is divided into parts, each of which has a coherent approach, but is not totally independent from the others. Part One serves as an orientation to the terms and basic techniques used in dealing with any Macintosh application. It is a good place to start if you haven't become conversant in Macintosh/Lisa software terminology and methods. Part Two explores the

Macintosh hardware in some detail and teaches general principles of computer operation. Part Three looks at the applications that are available with the dual goal of exposition and evaluation, and includes plenty of on-screen examples. Part Four evaluates various avenues for programming the Macintosh, and takes a close look at the system software that works the magic, the User Interface Toolbox.

Last, but hardly least, the Appendices deal with two areas that will be of concern to many Macintosh-watchers. Appendix A is a historical study that examines the conceptual lineage of the Macintosh over more than fifteen years of research. Appendix B is a hard-nosed comparison that pits the Macintosh against its archrival, the IBM PC. This should be of great interest to industry observers and nearly anyone considering a purchase in the near future.

Acknowledgements

Because this book was begun well before the release of the Macintosh, I had to rely upon the good will and talent of the staff at Apple Computer for much of my research. I would particularly like to thank Guy Kawasaki and Cary Clark for their aid in getting essential technical and background information. Martin Haeberli was very helpful concerning the AppleBus and AppleLine products. The staff at Microsoft Corp. was consistently friendly and gracious in supplying product information.

I would extend my warmest thanks to Jack Scott for his enthusiasm, friendship and graphic design expertise in handling the final production of the book. Sat Tara Singh Khalsa was a source of support throughout the project. I am very grateful for Joe Vojik's experience, typographical design and overall production guidance. At McGraw-Hill, Steve Guty cheerfully edited the manuscript and kept me honest. I would like to thank Byte Magazine for use of two of the photographs that appear in Chapter 17.

Completing this project gracefully under the pressures involved would have been literally impossible without the partnership and encouragement of my wife, Donna, who read the manuscript, prepared it for typesetting, and put up with my overwork. Gary McCabe was a port in the storm, a constant friend and counselor. Alan Pulaski provided his unfailing friendship and encouraged me to take on the challenge.

A Production Note

The text for the book was written using LisaWrite, and downloaded to an IBM PC with LisaTerminal and Crosstalk. IBM PC Wordstar was used to insert typographical macros. TelePhotronic, Inc., read the IBM Wordstar disks, and converted the macros to input suitable for their VIP typesetting machines. I would like to thank Tom Casper, President of TelePhotronic, for his warmth and his willingness to do what was needed to get the job done.

The illustrations for the book were prepared by the author using LisaWrite and MacPaint. They were printed on an ImageWriter printer and photostats were taken at various levels of reduction.

A Guided Tour
of the Desktop

This section will acquaint you with the basic terms and
techniques that are associated with the Macintosh desktop
software. It begins with an overview of the Macintosh
and its component pieces, and then introduces in turn the
mouse and each of the key areas of the desktop.
The chapters build on one another, bringing in new concepts
as they become appropriate. As is true of most of this book,
technical concepts are explained as they are introduced. When you
finish Part 1, you will be conversant in the basic methods that you need
to profitably use the Macintosh in your work and play.

Introducing the Macintosh

A Machine with Heart

When I first laid eyes on a Macintosh, in the Autumn of 1983, I was struck by the appeal of its small, light, cleanly designed package. Somehow, there was a feeling of implied power and grace about the machine that was evident before I ever sat down and used it. As I have gotten to know the Mac in work and in play, I've come to realize that what is unique about it is that it was built by people for people, and was not undertaken as just another adventure down some trendy technological alley.

This machine shows the hearts and souls of a very committed and bright team of designers, who were unwilling to compromise their vision of a powerful new personal computer that could be easily learned and afforded by a mass audience. I'm excited about what they've produced, and I hope to demonstrate in these pages why I think the Mac is unquestionably the finest product in its price range. Like anything else, it's not perfect, and I'll discuss its drawbacks as well. By the time you've finished, I think you'll have an excellent understanding of where the Macintosh came from, what it was intended for, and how it works.

Evolution

The Mac is clearly a product with a historical lineage, both in terms of hardware and software. The operating system is built around the idea of using a powerful graphics display to **simulate** real-world phenomena, such as folders, pencils, paper, and so on. This idea, often called the **desktop metaphor,** was refined in many years of research at Xerox PARC and elsewhere. A historical study in Appendix A shows exactly what the Macintosh has taken from its predecessors, and will help you understand why the desktop model was developed in the first place.

As a procedural note, if you're ever confused about a term that's used, you can probably find it in the glossary. This book is intended to serve anyone who wants to know more about the Macintosh, and does not require a technical background. When a particularly important term is used, it will be in boldface; most of these words will be included in the glossary.

Desktop Software

To begin with, we'll take a broad overview of the Macintosh and its features, and then explore the individual parts in more detail in succeeding chapters. The most important part of the Macintosh that the user sees is its software. This includes the **Finder,** which organizes the data on a disk into files, displays them as icons on the screen, and allows the user to manipulate them with the mouse. **Applications** are programs written by Apple and other vendors that function as tools, enabling the user to draw, paint, communicate, and perform other useful tasks. **Documents** hold the data that is managed by an application, and can be saved, copied or deleted. The **Desk Accessories** are small applications that can be used from within other applications, and perform convenient functions related to ongoing use of the Macintosh. Other **systems software** supports the functions of the Finder and the Desk Accessories, but is not seen by the user directly.

Under the Hood

Supporting the visible parts of the Macintosh are its very powerful hardware components. The Mac is built around the **Motorola 68000 16/ 32-bit microprocessor,** a very powerful device that is capable of minicomputer performance. It is supported by a small, select group of chips, including the **Zilog 8530 Serial Communications Controller,** the **6522 Versatile Interface Adapter,** and a custom Apple chip, the **IWM Disk Controller.** These are responsible for controlling various I/O (Input/Output) devices, including a **58-key keyboard,** an optional **numeric keypad,** a **mouse,** a ½″ **Sony microfloppy disk drive,** and two **high-speed serial interfaces.** The standard disks are capable of storing **400K bytes** each (400 times 1024 characters); if double-sided drives are produced in quantity, each disk will be able to store 800K.

The video display is a **512 by 342-dot bitmapped graphics display** under software control (see Appendix A) There is a **clock/calendar chip with battery backup,** as well as a **128-byte parameter memory** that retains convenience settings and the time when the power is off. At its release, the Macintosh came with **128K of RAM** (Random-Access Memory,) of which 80K is available for user applications. This will be upgraded to **512K** as soon as larger memory chips are available in quantity, which should be by early 1985.

All Macs have a **64K ROM** (Read-Only Memory), containing an extremely sophisticated array of systems software modules that applications can call. This is known as the **User Interface Toolbox,** and handles most of the overhead involved in using **windows, menus, icons, files,** and the other aspects of the Macintosh environment.

The Mac has a sound synthesis section that provides up to **four simultaneous voices** and **eight levels of volume** and has the capability to produce such complex waveforms as human speech. This occupies at most 50% of the processor's time, so that other computation can be carried out while the sound is being produced. There is an **external sound jack** that allows the sound signal to be sent to an external amplifier.

Packaging

The main cabihet is 13½″ by 8″ by 11″, and weighs only 17 pounds, not including the keyboard. A grip in the top center of the case allows the machine to be picked up and transported easily, and the **MacPack carrying case** (optional) fits the main unit, keyboard and mouse in a padded nylon bag for protection during transport.

The video screen is black-and-white, high-resolution, and measures 9″ diagonally. It has a very effective matte finish to reduce glare, and is extremely crisp and sharp. Connectors on the back (see Figure 1-2) support the mouse, external disk drive (optional,) two serial ports, external speaker, and 120 volt AC power line. An optional **programmer's switch** fits into the side of the cabinet, and provides a reset/interrupt capability if the machine is to be used for development. There are no hardware slots, and the cabinet is not intended to be taken apart by the user. Add-on peripherals can be assigned **virtual slots** and connected to the serial ports.

A Family of Peripherals

Figure 1-1 shows the Macintosh together with its family of add-on **peripheral devices.** Current Apple peripherals include an **external Sony 3½″ disk drive,** a **300 /1200 baud direct-connect modem,** and the **Imagewriter serial printer,** which is capable of printing all graphics that can be displayed on the screen. Tecmar and Davong have announced **add-on hard disk drives** that will attach to the high-speed serial ports.

Apple has promoted a close relationship with third-party developers and seeded some prototype machines to developers before release, resulting in a host of **hardware and software options** being available for the Macintosh within the first several months after its announcement. This policy should continue to pay off for the user, because well-informed developers build better products. This should also serve to develop momentum for the machine very quickly, which has a tendency to further fuel the flames as more developers become interested, and develop even more products.

Encouraging Third-Party Developers

As a developer, I am very impressed with the foresight of this strategy, because Apple's close relationship with third-party vendors will promote a wide variety of software and hardware add-ons. This will be essential for the Mac to survive in a very tough and competitive market. IBM, on the other hand, seems to go out of its way to ignore third-party developers when it comes to pre-release support, which inevitably produces its own

1.1   Macintosh and It's Family of Peripherals.

kind of results. Since the lackluster introduction of the PC/Jr and the birth of the Macintosh and the IIc, a significant amount of developer attention has shifted to Apple. This redirection of resources will have a delayed but profound effect in the marketplace when Mac projects start to come to fruition. There seems to be an automatic improvement in a product's design that occurs as a result of its fitting into Apple's very complete **User Interface Guidelines** for the Macintosh and the desktop environment. As a consequence, many products that were originally developed for the PC have gained a large measure of elegance and ease of use in the PC/Mac conversion process.

A New Lisa Family

Apple's co-announcement of the **Lisa II line,** with drastically reduced prices and full Macintosh compatibility, will further reinforce the market strength of the Macintosh because it creates a family with a clearly defined upgrade path. Mac buyers who need more horsepower can go to the Lisa without abandoning their software investment. Lisa was hailed as a technological breakthrough at its release, but its high price kept it out of the mainstream business world. Even with low sales numbers, Lisa had a profound impact on user interface design, spawning a number of "windowed" environments on machines that weren't designed for it. The new

Apple 32 family incorporates all of the strengths of the original Lisa, with improved software and at a much more attractive price point (see Figure 1-2.)

1.2   Macintosh and Lisa 2.

A New Standard

A unique feature of the Mac software environment is that all applications will share a common set of user interface standards that involve how people use the mouse, windows and menus (these terms will be explained in the next chapter.) Thus, much of the learning curve for a given product will have been absorbed by the first application that a person uses, because the techniques learned there will be directly applicable to any others that follow Apple's User Interface Guidelines. This favorably affects training time for any product that fits into the Macintosh standard.

Much has been said about the fact that the Mac is not MS/DOS compatible, meaning that it will never be able to run software developed for the IBM PC. Some industry watchers consider this decision to be a mistake, one that could seriously damage the Mac's marketability. They feel that it will exist as an isolated, stand-alone product, suffering from a lack of support from the thousands of PC-compatible products and vendors that now exist.

But consider how things were when the IBM PC was introduced. There were those who said the same thing about the PC in relationship to CP/M. One year later, those people were mute, because the PC had created its own standard in that time. If a product is good enough, it can do that—and it should, because anything else denies progress. I would rather have one simple, elegant word processor in the style of MacWrite or Macintosh Word than a thousand Wordstar imitators, all using different control keys and command sequences. The top software will be converted from the PC to the Macintosh environment, and in the process gain a much better user interface and dearly-needed consistency. The poor products, of which there are literally thousands, deserve to fade away (and undoubtedly will.)

The Macintosh is good enough to set is own standard and create its own market. It represents an advance in the personal computer state of the art, while the PC was a competent but very conservative restatement of what had gone before, even at its introduction. The question largely becomes whether Apple can salvage the credibility that was lost with two highly touted but poorly marketed machines in the Apple III and the Lisa I. Short of a major production disaster, my guess is that the Macintosh has a very bright future indeed, and may revolutionize the manner in which we conceptualize and actualize personal computing.

2

Of Mice and Menus

First Principles

This chapter and its successors in Part I will deal with how the features of the **desktop** are actually used. If you already own a Macintosh, this section will be a powerful aid to getting acquainted with the mouse, windows, menus, the Finder and its various components. This material will complement and give additional background to the excellent instructional materials provided by Apple. If you're just considering a purchase and want to find out more about the Mac Part I will allow you to see more directly what using the Mac is like, and point out some of the problem areas that you might experience. If you're one of the latter, you can use the illustrations as your practice screen when following the example.

When you first turn the Macintosh on, you will see a grey area with a number of rather interesting symbols distributed around it (see Figure 2-1.) This is the desktop that you've heard so much about. Just imagine yourself sitting at your desk: you might have a pad of drawing paper, a pad of writing paper, a trash can, a pile of scraps that contain bits and pieces of valuable information; you would have pens and pencils, empty folders, maybe a little 4-function calculator that you bought for $7.98, and if you're like me, probably some week-old coffee cups and a few cookie crumbs here and there. Well, cookies and dirty dishes haven't quite made it into the desktop environment yet, but the others are all there, if you look closely enough.

The symbols that you see are called **icons,** and they represent objects that you can use for various kinds of work and play. When you see something familiar on the Macintosh desktop, think about what you might use it for on your "real" desk. For instance, a pad of paper lends itself to having the top sheet torn off and written or drawn upon. After you're done, you might want to put it in a folder to keep it together with other papers on the same subject. When you work with the Macintosh, you'll find that the symbolic objects on the screen share many of the qualities of their real-life counterparts. A major difference is that to use the objects on your screen, you point to them with the mouse instead of manipulating them directly. At first this seems awkward, but it becomes second nature after some practice.

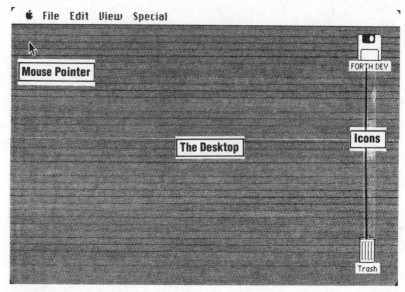

Figure 2.1 The Macinosh Desktop.

The Mouse and its Tale

Let's try using the mouse a little bit. You'll need a clear area on your desk that's about "eight by eight inches". Pick up the mouse, and hold it with its tail pointing away from you, with your index finger on the grey button. Now, slowly move it around on the surface your desk, and watch the arrow (or "pointer," for those of you who have hung around on desktops for awhile) follow the movements of your hand. You may find that the pointer changes shape when it's in certain areas of the screen. You will also find that you can't run the pointer off the screen, no matter how hard you might try.

It usually takes a little while before you can be very accurate in pointing with the pointer, but your ability will improve rapidly with practice. One trick that is good to learn early is picking up the mouse and centering it in a clear area of your desk if you find your hand wedged between your Mac and your old copy of War and Peace. The mouse doesn't do anything if it's off the desk, so you can always move it if you need more running room. Another nice feature of the mouse is its propensity for staying put if you're not using it. I usually leave mine pointing to an area of the screen that I might need access to often, or very quickly.

When using the mouse, you'll find that its motions correspond most closely to those of the pointer when the tail of the mouse is pointing more or less in the direction of the computer. If you turn it sideways, or point the tail toward you, the pointer will move in a different direction from that of your hand, which makes it rather difficult to be precise in pointing.

The pointer may take on different shapes in different parts of the screen, or while the computer is performing an operation that requires waiting. When you tell the Mac to start up an application, for example, the pointer will turn into something that looks like a wristwatch while it tends to the chores necessary to set up the program that you have requested. This means that you can't use the pointer to select anything until it looks like an arrow again. When the pointer is an arrow, there is a certain area around the tip of the arrow (called the "hot spot") that indicates exactly where you are printing. It is that area that you must position over an object that you are interested in. We'll cover that next. Whatever shape the pointer takes, the "hot spot" is generally in the most obvious part of the shape (such as the tip of a finger or an arrow.)

Menus

Now that you're on your way to mastering the mouse, let's try and do something useful with the pointer. Move the poiter to the icon that says "Empty Folder" beneath the picture. Now press the mouse button down once and release it. If we're both lucky, the Empty Folder icon will have darkened; that means that you've selected that particular icon. In general, work on the desktop involves **objects** and **operations.** First you **select** an object, then you **select** an operation. You selected the Empty Folders icon by pointing to it and **clicking** it once; now you can do something with it. Move the pointer to the word **File** at the top of the screen, and press the button down and **hold** it down. While you're holding the button down, move the pointer downward toward the bottom of the screen. As you pass the pointer over some of the headings, they turn dark, just as the icon did. The headings are all **operations,** (notice that they all sound like verbs), and will do something to the icon if you let go of the button while one of them is black. Try selecting the **Open** operation by letting go of the button while the **Open** box is black. It should blink briefly, and then the Empty Folder icon will blow up into a large white area on your screen (known as a **window.)** By **opening** the icon, you have indicated that you are interested in using the information represented by the icon. That operation will be covered more carefully in chapter 3; for now, go back to the file menu, but this time select **Close.** The white box will shrink back to its previous position on the desk.

What you have just done is use a **menu** to select an operation to be performed (see Figure 2-2.) The menu is the box that "pulls down" from the top line (called the **menu bar,)** sort of like a movie screen. Most of the time, the menus stay out of your way, because you don't want them cluttering up the screen and your brain. But as soon as you move the mouse near one of the menu titles, the corresponding menu will obediently pull down so that you can peruse its choices. You can roam freely among all of the menus as long as you hold the mouse button down, and nothing dangerous will happen unless you accidentally release the button while a menu option is selected. (And, in general, you would be asked for confirmation before anything really dangerous could happen, and could probably **UNDO** it anyway. More about that later.)

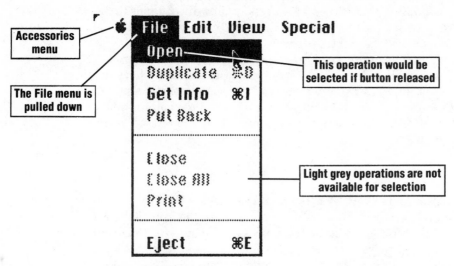

Figure 2.2 The File Menu.

The designers of the Macintosh have gone to great lengths to ensure that all applications will share common methods of operation. For instance, you will often see the same menu titles at the top of an application. The functions that they perform may change slightly, but the headings that are the same should work in the same manner. You can usually orient yourself very quickly by browsing through the menus and seeing what's available. For instance, the menu labeled **Edit** will show up very frequently in many different applications, but you will usually see the headings **Cut, Paste, Copy** and **Undo,** along with others that might be more specific to the application. But these four operations have a very clear and consistent meaning throughout the Mac environment. We'll cover editing in detail a little later.

More Mouse Techniques

For now, let's go back to the mouse. The mouse might seem to be a rather dull and unassuming little creature, but it can actually be quite versatile in the right hand. Either hand, for that matter. Go back to the Empty Folder icon with the pointer, and press and hold the button down.

From now on, when I use the word **"click,"** you can assume that I mean "push and release the mouse button". When I say **"press,"** I want you to hold the button down for some period of time. I'll be introducing some more terms that are useful as a kind of mouse shorthand as we go along.

Keep pressing, and move the pointer around on the screen. Now let go. The flickering box that followed the pointer around was a signal that you were **dragging** the Empty Folders icon to a different region on the desk. You can often move things around in this way, just like you can change the locations of things on a real desk. This technique is most powerfully applied to windows, but that, alas, must wait.

Now that you've made a miserable mess of your nice desk, we'll have to clean it up. Believe me, I understand the terror that this notion can inspire; there are parts of my desk that I haven't seen since the day I got it. But since we are now in the land of metaphor, cleaning up one's desk just isn't the job that it used to be. Move the pointer to the Special menu, and select the **Clean Up** choice. Not only will the Mac straighten up its own desk, it never complains about it! This technique is sure to get a lot of mileage at your next party—just move those icons around, go to Clean Up, and watch 'em dance.

One more thing about menus—you might have noticed that some of the headings were grey rather than black. If you tried to select one of the grey ones, nothing would have happened. Sometimes the designer of an application chooses to disable some of the choices on a certain menu, because they might be inappropriate. For instance, if you hadn't selected any icons, the Open selection on the File menu would have been disabled, because it wouldn't have known which icons to open. The creators of the Mac felt that this approach was better than simply removing the choice from the menu, because then things would be mysteriously disappearing and reappearing. If an operation that you would like to use is disabled, think for a moment about what information would be needed to complete the operation. This will usually lead you to something that you have forgotten. Sometimes, though, an operation will be disabled because the application was distributed without that part of it being functional, in which case you will find something in the documentation for that tool.

Do you recall the **Open** command that we performed from the file menu? Well, Open is such an important operation, the Mac's makers have included another, sneakier way to do it. Open is really only important when we start looking at **Windows,** but you should have this one under your belt before we go to the windows section. Now then... position the pointer over the Empty Files icon again. Click twice rapidly, and watch what happens! You have opened the icon by **double-clicking** it. This technique can often be used to do fairly common operations in the various applications; for instance, when editing text, double-clicking will usually select the entire **word** that the vertical bar is in.

One last trick before we leave mice and menus. Position the pointer somewhere in the middle of the screen, not on an icon. Now, press and move the pointer around on the desk. The rectangle that grows and shrinks, magically following the pointer, is called a **selection box.** With it, you can select a whole group of objects (not operations, though, because you can only perform one operation at a time.) You just have to fully enclose the objects that you would like to select in the box, and then release the button. All of the selected objects will darken. Select a group using this technique, and then position the pointer over one of the icons and drag it somewhere. Amazing! The whole crowd moves around like they're attached to each other with Crazy Glue. This is a fast way to rearrange objects on a cluttered desk, or to select a group of objects for the next operation.

Macintosh Mouse Techniques		
Term		**Description**
Click	*How*	Push button and release.
	What	Select an object or an insertion point.
Press	*How*	Push button and hold.
	What	Scroll slowly through text. Examine menus, drag icons and windows.
Drag	*How*	Press while moving the mouse.
	What	Move icons, change window sizes. Draw a select box around objects.
Release	*How*	Release the mouse button after drag.
	What	Confirm a menu selection. Mark the end of a selected group.
Double-click	*How*	Click twice in rapid succession.
	What	Open an icon. Select an entire word of text.
Shift-Click	*How*	Click while holding the shift key down.
	What	Accumulate selected items. Mark the end of a selected group.

Figure 2.3 Macintosh Mouse Techniques.

What's Next

If you play with the mouse for awhile, doing the things we've described, you'll find yourself becoming very comfortable with it as your primary means of talking to the Macintosh. After all, think about all the things you've already done without even touching the keyboard! Next we'll talk about windows and more sophisticated uses of the mouse and the desktop.

3

Windows

A Little History

Most personal computers use a relatively primitive arrangement by which a program can exchange information with you. When you start up a new application, it controls the entire screen, and has the ability to write characters anywhere on the physical screen. This works fine as long as you only want to do one thing at a time, because if two programs are using the screen simultaneously, they might end up fighting over the same area of screen.

People's lives, however, are usually not as simple as computer programmers might like them to be. For instance, I frequently need to see other documents while I am writing memos, letters or what have you; but I can only use my computer for one thing at a time (e.g., writing the memo,) so I have to print the other things out in order to be able to see them while I'm writing. But that takes so much time, I am actually tempted to make things up rather than print all of the other things that I need! Who knows how many lies are being told because of slow printers?

Well, this sad state of affairs prompted some visionary designers at **Xerox PARC** to come up with a better way of doing things. To begin with, they thought that you should be able to have more than one thing on your screen at a time, e.g., a memo, a graph, and part of a spreadsheet. While it is an improvement, this idea introduces even more problems, because you need an easy way to tell the computer which thing you want to work on, and to be able to switch back and forth between documents very easily. Using a keyboard for this purpose can lead to some very **non-intuitive** interactions with the program—you have to push keys that have no obvious relationship to the items on the screen.

The latter problem is adequately addressed by using a pointing device of some kind, such as a mouse. There can be very little ambiguity or confusion when you simply **point** to the document that you are interested in and push a button, as long as the different choices are clearly represented on the screen. This is far superior to using a keyboard to "describe" the operation that you would like accomplished.

The problem of representing the various documents on the screen is clearly not completely solved by just using a pointing device. How do the documents divide up the screen? Does the word-processor always get the top half and the spreadsheet the bottom? What if you want six things up there instead of two? These are the kinds of questions that drive system designers mad, and that most of us don't even think about. Well, the designers at PARC decided that the only way to avert total madness was to let the user decide what goes where, because how are they supposed to know where you want your damned spreadsheet? And with that decision came the conceptual birth of the **window.**

Windows

Windows are movable viewing areas that look into documents and other collections of information (such as disks.) Their sizes can be easily changed, and you can have several windows open simultaneously, overlapping or not, arranged to suit your needs. You largely control the way that your work is presented on your screen, just as you organize the work on your desk at home or in the office. Not so very long ago, home computing tended to present the following scenario: You were forced to accept the screen layout that a program's designer had created, and it was necessary to choose a single document to work on at a time, to the exclusion of all others; switching between documents probably required typing several memorized commands in the proper sequence, and there was a good chance that you could lose work if you forgot something. Also, it was likely that the different applications would have conflicting interpretations for the same command, meaning that you had to keep entirely separate rule books in your head for each tool that you used. (Or a stack of poorly-written manuals on your ungrateful "real desk".)

Window is a simple name for **virtual screen,** which is a complicated name for a method of making it appear to you like there are several screens on your computer instead of just one. You can change their sizes, overlap them, move them about, whatever looks best to you. A given application might use one or many windows to talk with you. The application doesn't care about where you've put them, how big they are, or anything else. If something that it wants to write won't fit in the window, it is simply cut off (clipped) where the edge of the window appears, or the document scrolls within the window boundaries so that new material is visible.

Windows make life easier for us by permitting each application to "think" that it is dealing with the entire physical screen, when actually it is using a subset whose placement and dimensions are controlled by the user. The mouse, menus and other features of the Macintosh desktop all contribute toward a consistent set of commands across all applications, because the emphasis is placed more upon pointing to objects that you can see than upon bizarre incantations that you have to remember.

Icons Open and Closed

The Macintosh uses windows for virtually all of its interactions with the user. The only time that you won't see any windows is when you have **closed** all of the icons on the desktop, and all that remains are the icons and the desktop itself. An icon can represent a number of things—applications, documents, folders, system files, and so on. When the icon is closed, you don't have direct access to the information contained therein. It's like having a book closed on your desk. But if you're interested in the object that the icon represents, you can **open** it, by double-clicking it or using the File menu. It then needs some way to communicate with you (a region of the screen,) so it blows up and becomes a window. Think of it as being like a microfiche reader; when not needed, it's just another object on your desk. But when you open it up and use it, you have a magic window to another world.

Let's look at a real example of a window on the Macintosh. You should have an icon on your desktop that looks like the outline of a Macintosh disk (see Figure 3-1.) This icon represents the disk that is currently inserted in

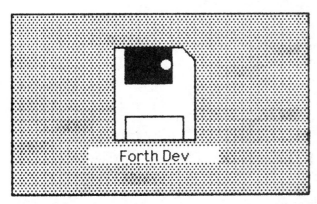

Figure 3.1   The System Disk Icon.

the drive, and can tell you information about all the things that you currently have stored on it. To ask it to reveal its information, you must first **open** it. (Just position the pointer over the icon, and double-click.) You will see a box come zipping out from the icon towards the center of the screen, and then enlarging into a white area surrounded by bars. You have just created a window that is used by the File manager. Here are some of the prominent features of a typical window: (See Figure 3-2.)

Title Bar

Windows always have a **title** in the top center of their region on the screen. The top quarter inch or so of the window is known as the **title bar.** This area is used for two things: Telling you what you are looking at and moving

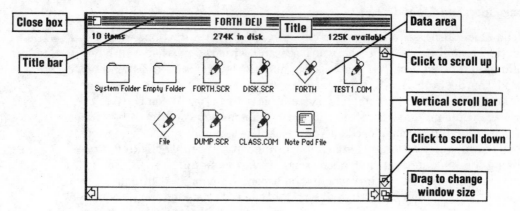

Figure 3.2　The System Disk Window.

the window around. When you **drag** the window by its title bar, you can move it to another area of the screen.

Close Box

Windows always have a small rectangle in the upper left hand corner, known as the **close box.** Clicking in this area of the window is one way to quickly close it and shrink it back down into its icon. (The other way is to use the File menu.)

Scrolling

Windows often have areas on the right and/or bottom that can be used to change your current position with respect to the information that the window is representing. These are called **scroll bars.** Imagine that you have a volume from an encyclopedia sitting with its cover closed on your desk. This would be like seeing the icon for the encyclopedia on your Mac screen, because you haven't opened it yet. Now open the book, (just like double-clicking the icon,) and you see two pages of fine print in front of you. But you really need only a small section of all of that information, and you would rather not be distracted by the rest of it, so you take a piece of cardboard and cut out a paragraph-sized rectangle from the middle of it. Now you can lay the cardboard over the book, and you will only see what is visible through the rectangle. If you need to see something later in the text, you can always move the cardboard down the page a bit. Notice that whatever text is behind the cardboard is simply cut off ("clipped" in windowspeak.) The cardboard is like a window on your Macintosh screen, only windows are a lot easier to use. They show you only a portion of the information which they contain, because you can't take in all of it at once anyway. The scroll bars move you around on the page behind the window, so that you can see other parts.

Changing Size

A crucial advantage to using windows is the ability to change their size. If a window has a box in the lower right corner that has a diagonal arrow inside of it, you can use the mouse to change the size of the window by dragging this size box around. To return to the cardboard analogy, it's as though you could change the dimensions of the cutout by simply grabbing a corner and pulling it toward or away from the center. Thus, a window needn't cover any area of the screen which you need for something else.

Active or Inactive

Lastly, windows can easily coexist with other windows on the same screen, although only one will be current (selected) at a given time. This means, for instance, that you could be using MacWrite to write a letter to one of your creditors on the bottom half of the screen, while looking at the Calculator desk accessory showing your checking account balances in the top half. This capability is enormously useful, and adds much to the power of the Macintosh desktop.

Managing Multiple Windows

Once you have opened several windows, you can switch between them easily by moving the pointer to an area inside of the window that you are interested in, and clicking the button. The scroll bars of that window will then become visible, indicating that the window is **current.** You will find that if you need to go back and forth between several documents, it will be much faster to keep them all open as windows than it would be to find their icons and reopen them each time.

Part of the reason for this is that when a window is open, the Macintosh keeps track of your current position within the window and the document, your currently selected display format, and so on. Selecting a different window merely determines where the Mac's main processor is going to put its attention; it doesn't lose the information that is specific to each window. So, if there is a particular section of a document that you want to keep going back to, the application will automatically put a "book mark" there when you make a different window the current one. If you were to close the window by clicking the close box and reopened it each time, chances are that you would have to do some scrolling to find the area that you were interested in, which would take time and attention away from the work that you really want to do. Note that not all applications allow you to open more than one document at a time, depending upon the memory requirements of the application.

When using multiple windows, a useful technique is something known as **tiling.** Visualize the roof of a house that has asphalt shingles. Each shingle is partially overlapped by others, but none are completely covered. Similarly, when working with several windows on the desktop, you have to be able to see any of the windows that you are interested in, so that you can move the pointer inside each of them. If you simply expanded the window that you were using to fill the entire screen, all of the others would be hidden from view when that one was "on top" (or current.) I have found that an arrangement like that shown in Figure 3-3 works best in most situa-

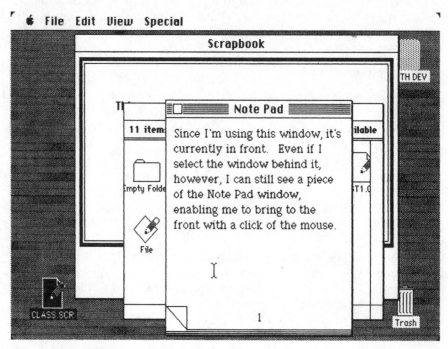

Figure 3.3   Tiling Multiple Windows.

tions. The most frequently used window is nearest the bottom, so that you can see the titles of the others when you are working with it. The least often needed window is at the top, and it will obscure the other titles when selected. The lower right hand corner and either the vertical or horizontal scroll bar of a given window will always be visible, so that you can conveniently select and scroll within it. The process is very similar to having a pile of papers on your desk, and shuffling the one that you need to the top. Try setting up three four windows in this manner and get a feel for how easy doing four things at once can be!

4

Editing and the Keyboard

The Keyboard

The Macintosh keyboard, with the exception of a few special-purpose keys, looks and acts very much like the keyboard on an average electric type-writer. It was designed chiefly to facilitate the entry of **text,** by which we mean any combination of letters, numbers and symbols (such as [,:,+,*, and so on.) On most computers, the keyboard must also serve as a means of entering **commands** (like telling the word processor to make a word **boldfaced.**) and moving the **cursor** around on the screen (a **cursor** being analogous to the **pointer** on the Mac.) Consequently, the keyboards on many other computers have a number of extraneous keys that have no-thing to do with entering text, such as function keys, arrow keys, an Escape key, and the like. As we have seen, the Macintosh has a mouse that can be used for virtually all commands and moving the pointer around, without having to remember what a lot of special keys are for. This allows the keyboard to be much simpler and to do what it was originally designed for over a hundred years ago: typing text.

There are a few keys on the Mac's keyboard that wouldn't be seen on your average typewriter, however. These include an "Option" key, a key near the lower left with a funny symbol on it that we'll call the "Command" key, and a key that says "Enter" on it. For the most part, these keys are there not because they represent the only means of doing something, but because they might represent a slightly faster means of accomplishing an action that is also available with the mouse. When working with text, since you already have your hands on the keyboard, it usually isn't convenient to keep moving your hand to the mouse and back, repositioning your hand over the proper keys each time. The designers of the Mac have tried to ease this burden by allowing many mouse actions to be imitated by pressing certain combinations of special-purpose keys on the Mac keyboard. We'll cover these in detail a little later, but first, let's talk some more about text.

Easy Editing

Using text on a computer can be divided into two phases: **Entry** and **Editing.** To enter text, you type it in on the keyboard and the Macintosh stores it somewhere—either in main memory, or on a disk. Being human, we don't always enter text correctly, and sometimes we just simply change our minds about the way something should look. On our old typewriters, the only option was retyping the page(s) that changed; in my case, I was much more likely to either try and find a gullible friend to do it, or to suddenly gain an appreciation for the old version (more frequently the latter.)

But now we have gullible computers that will obediently retype just about anything, for a price. Word processing programs vary widely in the difficulty associated with moving things around, deleting and inserting. Fortunately, the Macintosh provides a very elegant and easily learned model for editing text that you've entered in just about any application. In general, you first must **select** some text with the mouse, and then you select an **operation** to be performed on it from the **Edit** menu.

Natural Selection

When we talked about selecting things before, it was in relationship to icons, and was accomplished by **clicking** with the pointer somewhere inside the boundaries of the icon. This technique applies to text, as well. Within text, a **selection** can appear on the screen in two different forms. One is a blinking vertical line somewhere in the body of text, known as an **insertion bar.** The other occurs when an entire group of words or characters has a black background, meaning that you have selected that group of text.

The blinking insertion bar signifies that whatever you type on the keyboard will be inserted at the location of the bar, and the bar will be moved one character to the right. If there are existing characters to the right of the bar, they will all shove over to make room for the characters that you type. Text always behaves in this way on the Mac—whatever you type is inserted if there is a blinking insertion bar visible on the screen. The insertion point can always be moved by clicking the mouse with the mouse pointer in another part of the text. The insertion bar will suddenly appear at that point. If you click with the pointer beyond the end of the text that you have already entered, the insertion bar will appear just after the last character that was typed.

Some software on other computers has an "insertion mode" that can be on or off, implying that sometimes text is inserted, and sometimes it replaces what is already there. The state of this mode is often not clear, and it can lead to a lot of confusion, which is precisely what the designers of the Macintosh wanted to avoid. So there is no insertion mode on the Mac—text always inserts.

Group Selection

The second form in which a selection can appear is as a group of letters or words that has a black background. When this occurs, the entire group is selected, and if you were to type a character at this time, the entire selected group would disappear and be replaced by that character. You would then be left with the character you just typed, followed by the insertion bar. Any text to the right of the selected group would still be there, moving over to the right as you type. You can think of an insertion point as just being a selection of 0 characters. In this case, there are no selected characters to replace, so the new text is inserted without deleting anything first. This might sound rather confusing, but it will become much clearer the first time you actually do it. We'll get on to some real examples soon. For now, it will do to remember that whatever you type is going to replace the current selection, whether that selection is a group of text or simply the insertion bar; immediately after you have typed something, you will always have an insertion bar immediately following the character that was just typed.

There are two ways to select a group of text. One is to double-click, at which time the **word** that the insertion point is nearest will become selected. A word is defined as a group of letters or numbers without any intervening blanks or symbols—thus, if you double-clicked in a group of letters followed by a period, the letters would be selected, but the period would not. The second method of group selection is to **drag** the pointer through a group of text characters. The range of characters between where you started the drag and where you ended it would be selected. This method can be used to select an arbitrary range of characters, including symbols.

Text Fonts and Styles

The Macintosh provides a mechanism by which you can alter the **font** and **style** of text that you enter. A font is a set of characters that were actually designed by an artist, just as an architect would design a building. The artist specifies the slant and relative proportions of the lines in the characters, and tries to make the entire set fit together in an aesthetically pleasing manner. A font is completely specified by a name and a size, the size being in **points.** There are 72 points to an inch. For instance, this book is set in Century Schoolbook 10 point. This says that the design of the maximum 10 points from the bottom of the character that descends farthest below the line to the top of the tallest character.
est below the line to the top of the tallest character.

The **style** of text is separate from the font, being a method of modifying a given font. Examples of styles for text are **bold,** meaning that the characters are thicker and darker, italic, and underlined. On most computers, only one font is available, because it is fixed in hardware. Style differences are sometimes shown on these machines by varying the intensity of the characters, or underlining them. The Mac is able to provide many fonts and styles, because of the inherent flexibility in its graphics-oriented bitmapped display. Frequently, the font for a group of text can be changed simply by selecting the text and then choosing a font from a menu. Part III will cover some of the fonts available through the MacWrite and MacPaint applications.

The Edit Menu

Now that we know how to select text, let's look at the commands that are available for editing. Four operations will always be present (although they may not all be active) in the Edit menu. They are: **Cut, Copy, Paste** and **Undo.** The reason that some of them may not be active is that Cut and Copy always require a selection at least 1 character long to operate upon—an insertion point is like a selection of 0 characters, and wouldn't give those commands anything to work with. If you looked at the Edit menu when there was only an insertion point and no group selection, Cut and Copy would be gray, signifying that they were inactive.

In order to understand the edit operations, we need to introduce another part of the Macintosh desktop—the **clipboard.** This is an area that acts like a pile of clippings that you have taken out of a newspaper; it's a holding area for bits and pieces of documents that we might want to reuse. The clipboard is considerably more sophisticated than a pile of clippings, though. Once you put something in the clipboard, you can insert it again any number of times! It won't go away until it's replaced by another clipping. As you might have guessed, Cut, Copy and Paste move information into and out of the clipboard. Cut takes a selection, removes it from the document, and places it in the Scrap. **Copy** does the same thing without removing the selection from the document. Either operation will replace the current contents of the clipboard with the new selection. **Paste** copies the contents of the clipboard into the text, replacing the selection. If the selection is an insertion point, the clipboard contents will be inserted there. Paste, as we pointed out, never removes the contents of the clipboard—it only copies it back into the document, just as though you had typed the same text. Many applications include an item on the Edit menu that will show the current contents of the clipboard, which enables you to see what the results of a Paste will be.

The Real Thing

Allright, enough dry theorizing. These operations are really quite simple and obvious when you actually use them, so let's do it! Figures 4-2 through 4-4 will lead you through a series of sample editing operations; in order to use them, you must first open a tool that enables you to enter text, such as MacWrite or the **Note Pad** desk accessory on the Apple menu. To open Note Pad, you can move the pointer to the Apple menu, press the mouse button, move it down until the Note Pad line is selected, and release it. It would be a good idea to select **Show Clipboard** from the Edit menu first, so you can see how the clipboard is used during your editing session. When Note Pad comes up, you should see a window with a blinking vertical insertion bar in it (see Figure 4-1.) Whatever you cut or copy from the Note Pad text will appear in the Clipboard Window. Have fun!

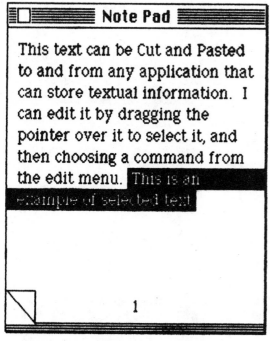

Figure 4.1   A Text Selection.

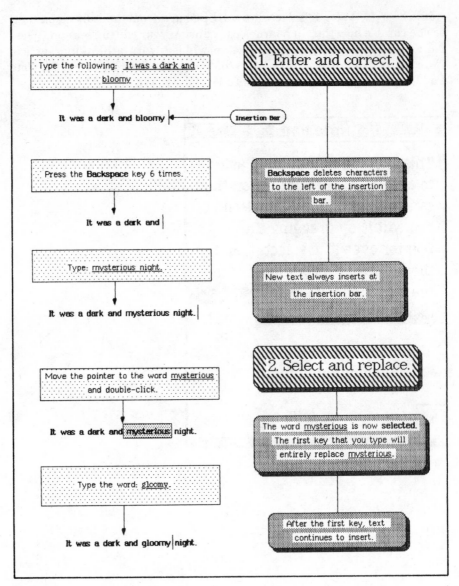

Figure 4.2

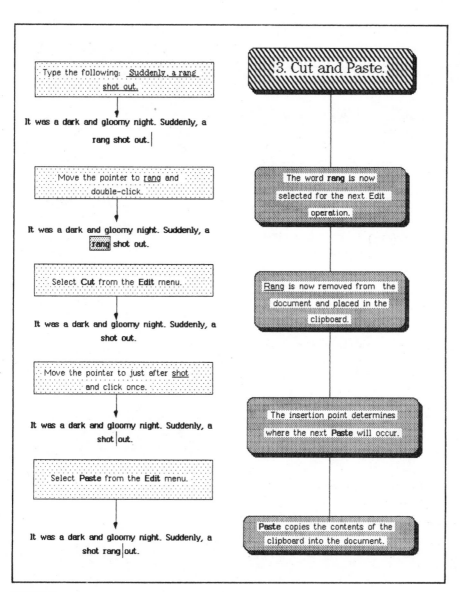

Figure 4.3

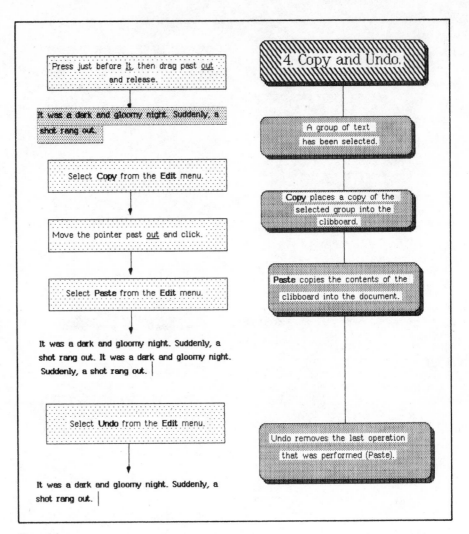

Figure 4.4

5

Dialogs

Mac and Thou

Occasionally, an application may require more information from you about your choices on how to carry out a certain task. An example might be a word-processing program that you have requested a print operation from; it might need to know how many copies you want, page size, line spacing, and related information that would not be available within the document itself.

Rather than requiring you to enter complicated command sequences, the Macintosh utilizes what are known as **dialog boxes** to allow you to enter this sort of information very directly. Dialog boxes look sort of like windows in that they are rectangular and overlay other things on the screen, but you usually can't change the size of a dialog box, and there aren't any scroll bars.

The most important fact about dialogs is that they are designed to represent information in a highly visual manner that allows you to make most of your choices by simply pointing and clicking with the mouse. Some dialogues exist principally to ensure that you have a certain piece of information before you proceed. Your only action in this case would be to acknowledge in some manner that you have received whatever communication the dialog is attempting to make. Other dialogs are there to request your choices and preferences, and involve a more complex set of actions on your part.

The definition of dialog implies that information will be exchanged in two directions. First, the application needs to tell you about the purpose of the dialog box, and what sort of response you need to make. To do this, it can employ text, icons, and other pictorial devices that have meaning within the particular application. Any text that is strictly "Mac to You", and not alterable by you in any way, will appear in the same font as the headings on the menu bar. This is known as the **"system font"**, and all applications will use it to convey system-related information to you. Secondly, the dialog may require some input from you, ranging from yes/no decisions to multiple-choice to text (what to name a document, for example.) To get this information, the dialog can use two kinds of items: **controls** and **editable text.**

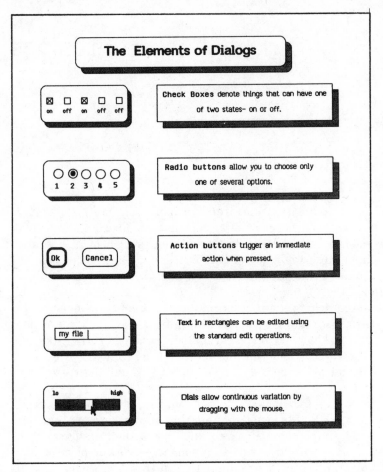

The Elements of Dialogs

☒ ☐ ☒ ☐ ☐
on off on off off

Check Boxes denote things that can have one of two states- on or off.

○ ◉ ○ ○ ○
1 2 3 4 5

Radio buttons allow you to choose only one of several options.

Ok   Cancel

Action buttons trigger an immediate action when pressed.

my file |

Text in rectangles can be edited using the standard edit operations.

lo   high

Dials allow continuous variation by dragging with the mouse.

Figure 5.1 Types of Controls Used in Dialogs.

Running the Show.

Controls are designed to allow applications to look like a very familiar part of our contemporary terrain: appliances. To most of us, there is a comfortable, reassuring quality around the common appliances that have been with us for years, like the radio in your 1955 Chevy that had a row of big black buttons, one for each station. It would seem that the trend of late is more in the direction of making cassette decks look like the flight panels of jet aircraft, but this is intended more to inspire awe than comfort. In general, it helps to have real buttons that you can see and push; at least you can quickly build a sense of mastery over a button, even if you don't have a clue about what the button does for the appliance. Contrast this to most personal computers. Without a manual, the only apparent invitation to button-pushing is the one that says "On/Off." But how do you persuade it to balance your checkbook?

Well, as a Mac user, you are the lucky owner of a complete set of genuine simulated buttons. When an application wants you to make a selection from a number of choices, it will show you a line of round or oval buttons that you can "push" by clicking with the mouse. Or, there might be a set of check boxes that you can either put a mark in or leave empty. These and other **controls** enable you to communicate with an application without knowing a special language or command set.

There are four broad groups of controls that you might see in Macintosh dialogs: (See Figure 5-1.)

1. **Check Boxes** are square in shape. They represent items that can have one of two states (such as On/Off, In/Out, Yes/No, etc.) A check mark means that a given box is in the "on", or "selected" state. This type of control is comparable to the On/Off switch on your television.

2. **Radio Buttons** are round. They represent a "multiple choice" kind of situation in which you can choose only one of several options. The obvious analogy is your car radio, in which you can hit one button, and the others all pop out. Within a group of radio buttons, only one of them can be "on" at a given time. This one will have a black dot in the middle.

3. **Action Buttons** are oval in shape, and when you hit one of them, the dialogue box will go away, because you have requested that it take some action. Frequently, one of these buttons will have a dark outline around it. This is the default button, and you can "hit" it by pressing the Return key as well as by clicking the mouse.

4. **Dials** can take on a variety of shapes. They are for settings that have a continuous range, like the volume setting on your television. You can change the position of a dial by positioning the pointer over the moveable section of the dial, and then dragging it to another position.

Editing Revisited

A dialog box may also ask you to enter text, such as the name of a document or folder. This sort of text is distinguished from system text by the following: It is in a lighter, smaller font, and it is enclosed by a rectangular box with square corners. A dialog may contain several editable text boxes. You can change the information in one of them by moving the pointer to it, clicking, and guess what? An **insertion** bar will appear. From that point on, the same rules apply as for any other editing situation (see chapter 4 for more information about editing.) You can replace words by double-clicking and entering new text. Cut, copy and paste may or may not be active, depending on the application.

Figure 5-2 shows a typical dialog box that has many of the components that we've talked about.

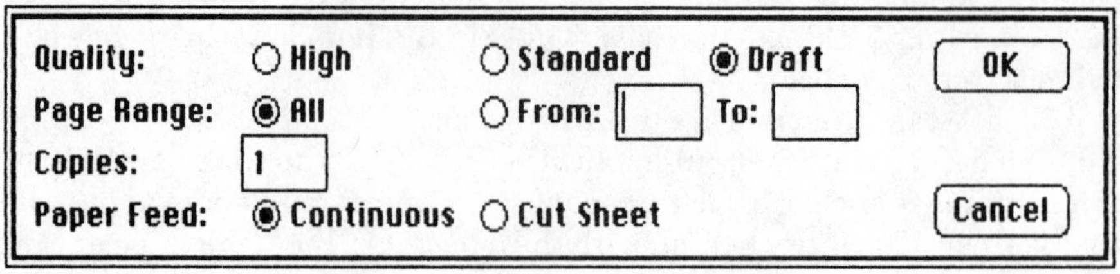

```
┌──────────────────────────────────────────────────────┐
│  Quality:       ○ High      ○ Standard   ◉ Draft    ┌──────────┐ │
│  Page Range:    ◉ All       ○ From: [   ] To: [   ]  │    OK    │ │
│  Copies:        [1      ]                            └──────────┘ │
│  Paper Feed:    ◉ Continuous  ○ Cut Sheet           ┌──────────┐ │
│                                                     │  Cancel  │ │
│                                                     └──────────┘ │
└──────────────────────────────────────────────────────┘
```

Figure 5.2   A Typical Dialog Box.

Tread Carefully

Alert Boxes are like dialog boxes, but have the chief purpose of issuing a warning or alerting you to a possibly undesirable consequence of something that you have requested. For instance, in an editor, if you had chosen to replace your document with an older version and discard your latest work, an **alert box** might appear. It would make sure that you really wanted to erase your work, and weren't caught up in a fit of artistic depression that you might regret later. Alert boxes contain only action buttons, e.g., one marked "OK" and one marked "Cancel". You would select Cancel if you wanted to retract your previous command, and OK if you wanted to go ahead with it. In this case, Cancel would probably have a bold outline, meaning that pressing the return key or clicking the button would result in cancelling your previous command. Usually the bold, or "default" button is the one that has the least disastrous results.

Alert boxes are distinguished by an icon in the upper left hand corner showing a talking head (the Macintosh spirit?) There are three types of alert, distinguished by what Mr. Mac is saying (see Figure 5-3.) An asterisk means a **Note** alert, which is basically just informational in nature. Your action is to acknowledge the alert by pressing the OK or Cancel button. A question mark signifies a **Caution** alert, meaning that you have chosen something that you might want to think twice about. This is the kind of alert that we just described, and will usually require you to make a Cancel/Continue decision. The third type of alert has an exclamation point, and is called a **Stop** alert. In this case, you have done something that either doesn't make any sense or is prohibited. Even user-friendly computers have their moods.

You will encounter dialogs and alerts frequently in your dealings with the Mac, and they soon will become familiar terrain. It's never pleasant to make a mistake or have the system encounter a problem, but it's refreshing to have the situation explained in easily understood language, with a clear statement of the choices that you can make. That's really what dialogs are all about.

Figure 5.3   Three Types of Alert Boxes.

6

Using Files

Whenever people handle large amounts of information, whether it is on a computer or on paper, they find it helpful to organize and group the information into smaller units. One common manual method is to place papers in envelopes or hanging files with easily visible name tags. This makes a given document much easier to find than if it were piled randomly in a stack of papers 6″ thick (a lesson learned from experience.)

Trees

Depending on how much information you have to deal with, you might have a few manilla envelopes, one for each broad category of information (like money, love letters, insurance papers, etc.), or you might further subdivide each broad category into smaller, more specific sections. For instance, broad category money could be divided into bills, investments, checking account, budget, and other finer categories. If you continue this process, you will end up with a lot of extremely detailed and specific groupings for your papers, with groups of these categories each collected under a more general heading. If we drew a picture representing this arrangement of information, we would see a structure somewhat resembling a tree (See Figure 6-1.)

Researchers who have studied the ways that people organize information have found that this kind of tree-like structure is very common and also quite powerful. Its power stems from the fact that we all sort of naturally tend to subdivide things in our brains as our chief method for understanding complexity. It is much easier for us to assimilate new facts when we can group them with other facts that we have previously stored in our memory. Computer scientists call this tree-like grouping of data a **hierarchy.**

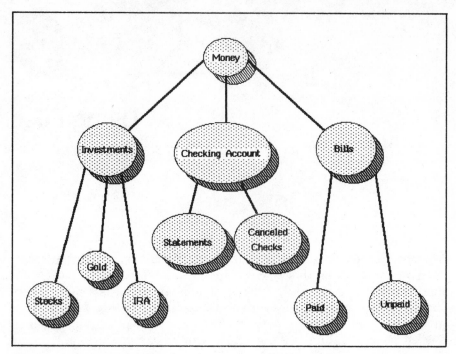

Figure 6.1 A Treelike File Structure.

Getting Organized

Let's look at how a typical hierarchical filing system might appear in real life. For the broad and very important category, money, we will reserve an entire drawer in our filing cabinet. Within this drawer, we will place some large hanging files that can hold a number of folders each. We will name these hanging files according to the next level groups under money—investments, checking account, etc. Within each hanging file, we will place a number of folders; for instance, under investments we might want to have stocks, bonds, gold, and any other investments that we were involved in. Finally, each of these folders would contain actual documents relating to the category of the folder.

Fine, now what does this have to do with the Macintosh? Well, the Macintosh, like many other computers, has a disk drive that can be used to store information magnetically. How this actually occurs is rather mysterious to most people; for now, we'll just say that all of the text and drawings that you can prepare using Mac applications can be stored on the disk and retrieved again for later editing.

Computers in Disguise

A funny thing about computers is that they often try very hard to look like something else—a piece of writing or drawing paper, for instance. In fact, you could say that a good way to assess the quality of a computer is this very principle: To what degree does it look like something other than a computer, something that you can really use in your everyday life? A computer that just looks and acts like a computer is a fine thing if you happen to be a programmer. But most of us would rather have a tool that can help us do word processing, drawings, spreadsheets and other practical tasks.

There is a subtle distinction being made here between two different ways of looking at machines like computers. One is the **logical** view and the other is the **physical** view. Here's the difference: If you got up close and took a good look at a television screen, you would see a lot of little tiny glowing dots of light. These dots are produced by electrons hitting a substance on the back of the screen that glows when hit. This is the physical view of your television. It is important, in fact essential, if you want to build a television set yourself or explain how it works to someone else, but it really has very little impact on your enjoyment of the programming on the television. When you step back and all of the dots merge into a coherent, moving picture that conveys stories about people, you are taking the **logical** view of the TV, and you see it as an entertaining window into another world.

The Logical Mac

One of the things that the Macintosh does well is present a very coherent and easily understood logical view. For the most part, the Macintosh looks like things that we use in our everyday life—paper and pens, a desk, and as we shall see, files and folders. The physical view of the Mac for most of us is not very relevant—we know that there is an extremely complex system working behind the scenes to make things simple for the user. In order to understand and use files, though we need to delve a bit into the physical side of things, because it is very helpful to be aware of some of the constraints imposed by the physical implementation of the filing system.

Disks, Bits and Bytes

The Macintosh uses a Sony 3½″ "micro-floppy" disk drive to store all of its documents and tools. Early models of the Mac use single-sided disk drives, and a double-sided version is anticipated when the drives are available from Sony. A single-sided drive only has one head that can be used to read or modify the magnetic data on the disk; consequently, you can only store information on one side of the disk, and are limited to half of its capacity. (The disk can't be flipped over like a record). Later models have two heads, and can use the entire storage capacity of the disk.

Double-sided drives can store approximately 800,000 characters of data on the disk, and single-sided drives 400,000. That sounds like all the grains of sand on the beach, but how much is it really? Well, if we're talking about text, each letter, number, space and symbol take up one character on the disk. This book, for example, would occupy about 200,000 characters, and theoretically, you could fit about two copies of this book if you typed it in using MacWrite on a single-sided Mac disk (It was actually typed in by yours truly on the Lisa word processor, LisaWrite). I said theoretically because you can do special formatting things on word processors, like **boldface** or underline, that take up more room when stored with the document. In addition, the Mac disks that you will be using will have **tools** stored on them (applications such as MacWrite, MacPaint, and so on) as well as information that the system needs to keep track of what you have stored on the disk. So the amount that you can actually store will be a good bit less than 400,000 characters.

Every piece of information that a computer uses—text, drawings, in fact,even its own "brain", reduces to a bunch of numbers. A computer without those numbers stored in it is deaf, dumb and blind—it has no instructions about what to do next and no way to communicate with the world to get any instructions. But how are the numbers stored? One simple way to represent numbers is as an ordered sequence of on/off states (see Figure 6-2.) This is known as "binary arithmetic," and is the basis upon which all modern "digital" computers are built. Many things in the physical world have the ability to exist in two states, which is all that is needed to store a binary number. For instance, imagine a tray of ice cubes in which some of the ice cubes have melted to form water. We see a physical substance, water, in two different states, solid and liquid. If we assigned a number to each combination of solid and liquid cubes in the tray, then we would have a device for storing binary numbers (eventually, though, all of the cubes would melt, and then we would just have a big puddle.) Computers exploit substances other than water as media for storing binary numbers on a very tiny level, so small that hundreds of thousands of numbers can now be stored on a silicon chip smaller than your fingernail.

Disks also contain substances that can be made to exist in one of two states. The usual technique is to spread a lot of very fine iron oxide particles on the surface of the disk that can be magnetized in one of two directions. It takes eight of these particles to form the smallest unit that computers generally work with, known as a byte. Each particle forms one binary digit, and the eight together can store numbers between 0 and 255. Text is stored by assigning one of these numbers to each different character that you might enter at a keyboard; "A", for instance, is assigned the number 65. All of the characters that you typically would need have been assigned a standard set of number codes, known as the Ascii codes (see Figure 6-3.)

Because the Mac uses the Ascii system for storing text, it will be able to communicate with many other computers, and exchange text with them. First, though, a software author will have to create a tool for this purpose. You couldn't simply take a Mac disk and put it in the drive of another machine, and expect to be able to transfer any data; for one thing, the disks are probably a different size (not many other computers use the 3½" drives

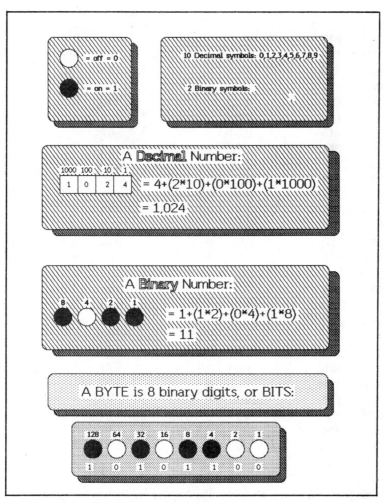

Figure 6.2   Binary Arithmetic.

yet,) and for another, the way that the data is physically **organized** on the disk is proprietary to Apple, and unique to the Macintosh operating system. (The entire Apple 32 line shares a common disk format; see Part II.) So a communications program would first read the data from the disk into memory, and then transfer it either over a phone line or via cable to the other machine. Once the data is off the disk and in memory, it looks like any other textual information encoded by the Ascii convention. Apple has developed a communications program for the Macintosh, MacTerminal, which enables it to operate like a DEC VT100 terminal (see Part III.)

Finding Yourself

If we just used the disk as one big jumble of text, though, we would be no better off than we were with the big stack of papers (in fact, worse off,

000	NUL	043	+	086	V
001	SOH	044	,	087	W
002	STX	045	-	088	X
003	ETX	046	.	089	Y
004	EOT	047	/	090	Z
005	ENQ	048	0	091	[
006	ACK	049	1	092	\
007	BEL	050	2	093	]
008	BS	051	3	094	^
009	HT	052	4	095	_
010	LF	053	5	096	`
011	VT	054	6	097	a
012	FF	055	7	098	b
013	CR	056	8	099	c
014	SO	057	9	100	d
015	SI	058	:	101	e
016	DLE	059	;	102	f
017	DC1	060	<	103	g
018	DC2	061	=	104	h
019	DC3	062	>	104	i
020	DC4	063	?	106	j
021	NAK	064	@	107	k
022	SYN	065	A	108	l
023	ETB	066	B	109	m
024	CAN	067	C	110	n
025	EM	068	D	111	o
026	SUB	069	E	112	p
027	ESC	070	F	113	q
028	FS	071	G	114	r
029	GS	072	H	115	s
030	RS	073	I	116	t
031	US	074	J	117	u
032	SP	075	K	118	v
033	!	076	L	119	w
034	"	077	M	120	x
035	#	078	N	121	y
036	$	079	O	122	z
037	%	080	P	123	{
038	&	081	Q	124		
039	'	082	R	125	}
040	(	083	S	126	~
041	)	084	T	127	
042	*	085	U		

Figure 6.3   The Ascii Codes.

because it's tough to search through a pile of iron oxide particles). The Mac operating system has built into it a hierarchical filing system, sort of like the one we dreamed up for the financial papers. Only the system is there, however, not the actual information—that's for you to provide. It's as though you had a file cabinet with a lot of empty folders and labels ready for your papers, but there's a difference—you also get a free secretary to keep track of everything so you don't lose it! (Called, appropriately enough, the **Finder.**)

All information on the Mac disk is organized into **files.** Files are the basic units, the atoms of the disk operating system. A file is a (not necessarily physical) grouping of data on the disk with a common name. A file may have different parts scattered around on the disk, and the operating system keeps track of all of the parts with a separate area of the disk, known as a **directory.** The directory stores important information for each file—its name, where the parts are located, when it was created, who owns it, and so on.

All the World's a File

Files need not be text or drawings—they can also hold applications and system programs; even the Finder itself starts out as a file before it gets loaded into memory when you turn the Mac on. Most of the time, the only files that you will be interested in will be **documents**—special files that are used to store your work from a particular application. Files relate more closely to the **physical** view of the computer, while documents are mostly **logical** entities that are part of the way you do your work.

The next level up from files in the physical ordering of the disk is the **volume.** Each of your Macintosh disks has a volume, which allocates space on all or part of the disk and serves to identify the disk to the operating system by its volume name. The volume name consists of from one to 27 characters, followed by a colon (:(. The volume contains a directory of all of the files that are stored on it. Volumes can be **mounted** or **unmounted**—a volume is mounted when it is placed into the internal or external disk drive and the operating system reads the information about the volume into memory. Figure 6-4 summarizes the relationship between disks, files and volumes.

What most personal computers provide in terms of a filing system is what we have just described—the ability to produce files and store them on a disk. A "traditional" operating system (like CP/M or MS/DOS) also provides commands (such as PIP a:=b:*.*) for copying, removing and performing other operations on files. This part of computing is usually the hardest for a newcomer to learn, because it has no analogy in previous experience—an entirely new set of concepts and command sequences must be learned. The Macintosh drastically reduces learning time with respect to file operations by integrating them into the desktop scheme, which is largely visual and dependent upon simple operations like pointing. As we

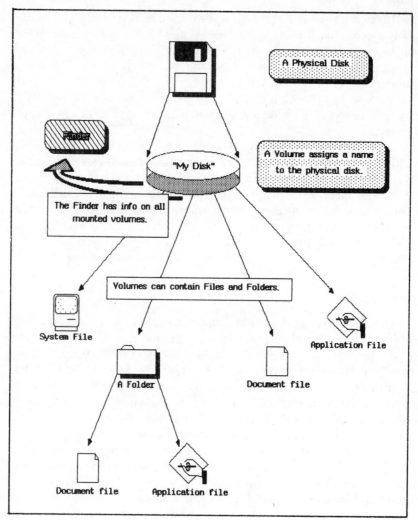

Figure 6.4   Disks, Files and Volumes.

pointed out before, the "Open File" operation can be achieved by simply pointing to an icon and double-clicking.

Filing Made Easy

What the Mac's designers have done is "hidden" the concept of files by representing them as objects on the screen (icons) that can be directly manipulated with the mouse. The only files that most users need to manipulate are the **documents** that they use with the various applications; these have obvious-looking icons, like sheets of paper.

What sort of operations do you need to perform on files? The primary ones are to create a **new** file, to **open** an existing file so that you can use it,

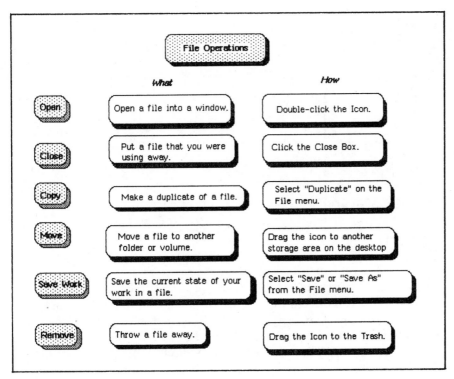

Figure 6.5   File Operations.

to **close** a file that you are using (put it away), and throw an existing file away. Figure 6-5 summarizes the various operations that can be performed on files, and how they can be accomplished. You will notice that the most common operations (Open, Close, Remove) can be performed with the mouse alone, while the others, needed less often, are only available from the **File** menu. This is no accident—in general, the Mac is designed so that the great majority of the operations in the different parts of the desktop can be accomplished using only the mouse and the objects that you work with (icons, text and drawings.) The menus are there to support additional functions that are essential to the application, but required less often.

File Operations in Depth

Now let's go over the various file menu operations in a little more detail. This discussion will cover the general case —not all applications will provide all of these options, and some may provide additional ones. This set, though, will give you a good understanding of the various kinds of things that you can do with files and some of the standard ways of handling file-related information. Figure 6-6 shows a typical application's file menu.

▪ **New:** When you want to start from scratch in an application, and create a new document, selecting **New** on the **File** menu will create a document

Figure 6.6   An Application File Menu.

window with "Untitled" in the title bar. "Untitled" is not a real file name—you will be asked to give the document a different name before you can save it permanently on the disk. Acceptable filenames can contain any of the characters available on the keyboard except for colon (:) (colon is used to identify volume names, and could cause some confusion.) A filename can be from 1 to 255 characters long including spaces; thus you could have a file with a title like "A comprehensive listing of at least 50% of the people who have sent me > 3 Christmas cards, and to whom I have never sent any, to my eternal detriment." If you already have a document open and the application can only use one document at a time, "New" will be disabled (it will appear in light gray on the menu.) If this is the case, you must Close the current document first.

- **Open:** When using an application, this selection from the File menu will put up a dialog box containing a list of all of the files that can be used with

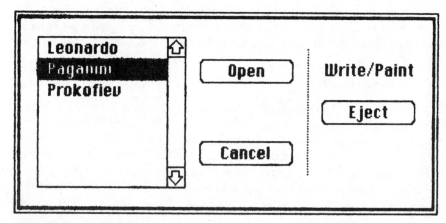

Figure 6.7   The Open Dialog.

the application (see Figure 6-7.) The box will contain the following action buttons: **Drive** allows you to switch from the internal to the external drive, or vice-versa (note: this button will not appear if you only have one drive on your Mac); **Eject** will allow you to change disk volumes within a given drive; **Open** will open the file (only one) that you have selected from the list. If there is a problem loading the file, you will see an Alert box describing the problem. If the file opens successfully, it will blow up into a document window with the name of the file in the title bar.

- **Save:** When in an application with an open file, Save will attempt to save your work out to the disk by writing over the old copy of the file. If you are working with a document that has "Untitled" in the title bar, Save will prompt you for the name that you wish to save the document under, as in **Save As,** below. It is good to use the Save command every fifteen minutes or so when working in an application, because then if something bad happened to your Macintosh, you would only lose fifteen minutes of work at the most.

- **Save As:** This option will bring up another dialog; it functions in exactly the same manner as Save, except that it prompts you for the name of the file that you would like to save your work under rather than assume that you want to use the name currently in the title bar. If the filename that you specify already exists, you will be asked whether you really want to overwrite the file on the disk, since this would lose any information that was previously in the file by replacing it with your current work in the application. Save As can be used to make multiple backup copies of your work by changing disks and saving the file again, or just keeping two copies on the same disk. Backing up a file (copying it) to two disks is safer, because then if one disk became damaged, you would be able to recover your work from the other copy. Once the save has occurred, (by pressing the **Save** action button), the name in the title bar will change to match the name that you have entered.

- **Close:** The "front-most" (active) window on the screen, whether it is a dialog, desk accessory, or document, will be closed and put away. If it's a document, you will be asked if you would like to save your work first, and then the file will be closed. Some applications disable all file menu items when a desk accessory is active, requiring you to explicitly close the accessory using its close box before you can use the application.

- **Print:** Although not really a file command, print is usually put on the file menu if there isn't a separate Print Menu. This option will bring up a dialog box that will enable you to set up the proper parameters for your printer: the page size, final or draft quality, and so on. Some applications might also provide a Page Setup item that allows additional parameters to be altered.

- **Revert to Saved:** If you wish to discard the work that you have done since your last Save, you can choose to **Revert** to an older copy of the file. This will clear your current work from the application, and replace it with the contents of the file having the name specified in the title bar of the active window. This is one of those commands that could lead you to take up another career if you made a mistake with it, so you will see a dialog box that asks if you're "sure." If you have trouble with big decisions, this probably isn't the command for you.

- **Quit:** Is how you leave an application. A dialog box will ask you if you really want to quit, and then you will be asked if you want to save each open file that you have modified. The choices on the buttons will be "Don't Save" and "OK."

Folders are a special kind of file that allow you to collect a group of files, including other folders, together rather than leave them all out on the desktop. You can place a document or application into a folder by dragging it into the immediate vicinity of the folder with the mouse, and then releasing the button. To see the contents of the folder, you simply double-click in it, and it will become a window displaying its contents. Folders allow you to create the hierarchical filing system that we discussed very easily. To create a new folder, double-click the "Empty Folder" icon, and a new folder icon will appear on the desktop. You can name it by positioning the pointer in the the icon's name field and typing your chosen name; standard editing protocol is followed when you enter the text for the name.

The **View** menu allows you to determine how the folder will display its contents to you. The default arrangement is **By Icon,** which causes the folder to display all of its documents and applications as icons. **By Name** will display the contents as line items, organized alphabetically by filename. This option might be easier to use if you have a lot of icons with similar names. **By Date** displays objects in the order that they were created, with all documents grouped together. This would be useful, for example, if you created a status report each week and didn't want to encode the date in the name. **By Size** and **By Kind** group the files according to those characteristics.

File management is often the most confusing aspect of computing for many people. The Macintosh removes most of the mystery from file operations by replacing long command sequences with direct, visual manipulations of objects. I would suggest taking a blank diskette and playing with files using one of the Macintosh applications, so that you can get the feel of how things work before your real data is on the line. If you have a single drive system, you will find that, in order to create a new diskette, you will have to endure many, many swaps of diskettes in and out of the drive. This is because the Mac stores limited chunks of the diskette in memory at a given time, and it must use memory to hold the data that is being copied from one disk to the other. For this reason, I think many people will feel compelled to purchase another drive, but those who can't afford it will just have to bite the bullet until they can. Also, disk space runs out quickly. By the time that all of the necessary system files are included on a MacPaint disk, for example, there is only around 100K available for storing user data.

It is relatively easy to use a disk for "data only" with MacPaint and MacWrite; this means that you wouldn't place any of the systems files on the disk, but would store only documents that could be used with the applications. You would then boot an application from its disk, select Open (which will bring up the Get File dialog,) hit the eject button, and insert your data disk. The window will list all of the files on the data disk appropriate to the application, and you can select one and open it. You might have to endure a couple of swaps to load your file, but at least you can store a good number of documents on one disk using this method.

Copying files between disks is accomplished by ejecting a disk, inserting a new one, and then dragging the desired file icons to the new disk and releasing the mouse button. If several files are to be copied, it will be much faster if you select them as a group and move them together to the new location. The Macintosh Owner's Guide provides detailed information on copying files between disks, and is worth several visits before you start.

The Desk Accessories

Gadgets for the Electronic Desk

The **Apple** menu, in the upper left-hand corner of the screen, provides you with several "mini-applications", known as **Desk Accessories.** Some of them are for setting up system parameters, some are generally useful, and some are just for fun. (See Figure 7-1.) These can all be run while you are in

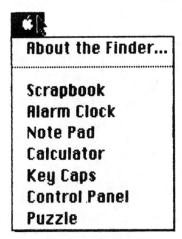

Figure 7.1   The Apple Menu.

the middle of a Macintosh application. Normally, two applications cannot be run at the same time, because the Mac's memory only has room for a single application. The Desk Accessories, though, are stored in a special area of memory that is reserved especially for them, so they can be used at almost any time (that is, whenever the Apple menu is present on the menu bar.)

When you start a desk accessory, it will create a window for itself on the screen, its size dependent upon the accessory. If you are using an application when you start the desk accessory, the application's window will become inactive (its scroll bars will become light outlines,) and the desk accessory will be in front of any other window on the screen. If you don't wish to use the desk accessory just then, but want it to remain on the screen (an example would be selecting the alarm clock and keeping it around just so you would know what time it is,) you can resume using the application by clicking within its window. The accessory will stay on the screen, although it might be overlapped by the active window. You can move the accessory's window by dragging within its title bar, and place it somewhere conveniently out of the way. Some applications, such as MacPaint, require you to close any open desk accessories before returning to the document. This is due to the memory requirements of the application.

When you're done using a desk accessory, you can close it by clicking its close box or by selecting **Close** from the file menu while the desk accessory is active (when its window is in front of everything else.) It will then disappear, and can be re-invoked at any time by selecting it from the Apple menu again.

You can have several desk accessories on the screen at the same time, all coexisting with an application. Because some of the accessory windows are rather large, however, you wouldn't be able to see everything at once, so it probably wouldn't make sense. The photographs in this chapter all show several desk accessories active at the same time (see Figures 7-2 to 7-4.) Let's take at a look at some of the things that the desk accessories can do.

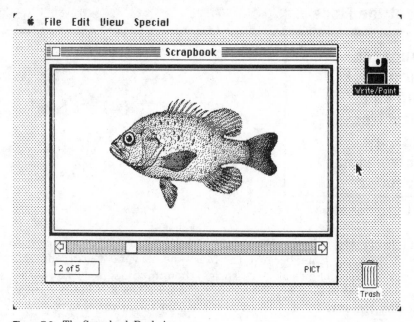

Figure 7.2   The Scrapbook Desk Accessory.

The **Scrapbook** (see figure 7-2) is a "billboard" that can display anything that you can get into the Clipboard—text, pictures, or numbers. You
can use it as a place to put favorite MacPaint drawings, poems, love letters,
and whatever else your heart desires. The only trick is that you must use
the Edit commands: Cut, Copy and Paste to get your little gems into the
Scrapbook. That is, you have to Cut or Copy from somewhere else and Paste
it into the Scrapbook. The "somewhere else" can be MacPaint, MacWrite,
another application, or even another desk accessory! Each time you paste
into the Scrapbook, you start a new "page". You can then browse through
the pages by using the scroll bar at the bottom. The data that you paste into
the Scrapbook is actually stored on disk in the "Scrapbook File". This is a
good place to collect those little pieces of drawings or text that you didn't
really want to throw away—any time you put something into the clipboard, you can select Scrapbook and Paste it in for safekeeping. (But remember that disks, like closets, fill up sooner or later, which would point
out a need for a "garage sale" desk accessory.)

The **Calculator** (see Figure 7-3) is a four-function calculator that really
works! (I think it's also a hands-down winner for the thinnest calculator
ever made.) This one is pretty self-evident, so I won't waste my printer's
valuable ink telling you how to use it. Once you master the fact that you
have to use the mouse to push the buttons and can't press the screen with
your fingers, you're home free.

The **Alarm Clock** (see Figure 7-3) allows you to wake yourself up if you
happen to nod off during a long computing session. It's also handy if you

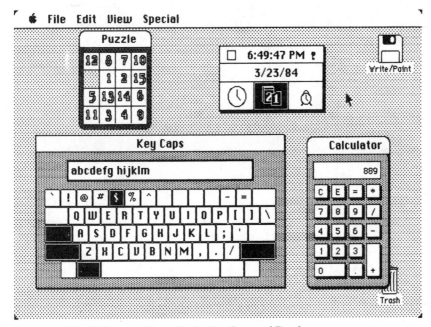

Figure 7.3   The Calculator, Alarm Clock, Key Caps and Puzzle.

like to take your Mac to bed with you at night (they're good at keeping your feet warm, but don't expect much in the way of conversation.) You can set an alarm to go off at specified date and time, and it's also nice to leave around on the desktop as a clock.

The **Key Caps** desk accessory is a miniature typewriter that shows you what characters the keys can produce in the different modes (normal, shifted, and option.) Holding the option key down produces specialized graphics characters, as Figure 10-3 demonstrates. What you type appears in a small window at the top, which can then be Cut or Copied into the clipboard.

The **Puzzle** (see Figure 7-3) is a little plaything for those times when you can do little else but mindlessly push numbers around. It's a good example of how effectively the Mac's graphics can simulate a real-world phenomenon.

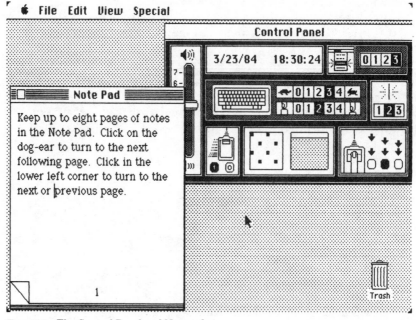

Figure 7.4 The Control Panel and Notepad.

The **Notepad** (see Figure 7-4) is a multiple-page holder for text that you type or paste into it. Notepad has a novel method of page turning—you move the pointer to the part of the page that looks like a turned up corner, and the Mac does a cute simulation of a page turning. Fortunately, you don't have to lick the mouse first. This accessory is a marvelous example of the power in simplicity.

The **Control Panel** (see Figure 7-4) is a wonderful little window that looks like an amusement park. With this accessory, you can adjust system parameters that keep their value even when the Mac is turned off. (That's why the battery is in the back.) Using the control panel, you can make certain aspects of the Macintosh desktop behave according to your preferences. These include speaker volume, time, date, menu selection flashing, the rate of blink of the text cursor, the pattern displayed in the desktop, how much time is allowed between double-clicks, how fast the mouse pointer moves in relation to the physical mouse, and keyboard repeat rate. I challenge you to find another creation of man (or woman) that clearly conveys a method for and allows you to change that many things in a 2″ by 3″ square.

The desk accessories contribute much to giving the Macintosh its unique character, and demonstrate beautifully how a picture is worth many more than a thousand words. Apple is likely to release additional desk accessories in the future, and they are making known the mechanism by which third-party developers can build their own. I am looking to this area for some really exciting things, like miniature music synthesizers, drawing pads, and the like.

Onward...

Well, it's a wrap for our tour of the desktop. I hope that you learned something, or at least were stimulated enough to find out more. Using the desktop is likely to be a trial-and-error sort of thing for awhile, but that's what the Mac was designed for. Next, we'll take a close look inside the Mac, and see what makes all of its fancy software tick.

Inside
the Macintosh

Supporting the powerful desktop software is a much less
visible part of the machine—its hardware devices. The Macintosh
hardware design is an exercise in efficiency and simplicity.
This part of the book will explain in both general and specific
terms how the Macintosh hardware functions, and will discuss
some of the relative merits of Apple's approach. General
principles of computer technology will be introduced as they
are needed to provide background and understanding.

8

The Central Processor
and Support Devices

The brains of any computer can be found in the CPU chip, or **Central Processing Unit.** This chip, more than any other single factor, determines how fast and how easily programable a computer will be. Early microcomputers were built around the 6502, 6800 and 8080 CPUs, which were all 8-bit computers. The 8 refers to the length of the largest number that the computer can move in or out of memory at one time. An 8-bit number can range between 0 and 255, which is not large enough to handle typical quantities that would arise in everyday work. In order to handle larger quantities, the computer must break things up into many separate operations on small numbers, which takes much longer than it would if it were a single operation.

A CPU has storage bins, like buckets, inside of it that it uses to hold numbers that it is working on. These buckets are called **registers,** and are typically 8 or 16 bits in length. Even 8-bit processors sometimes have one or two 16-bit registers, for convenience in handling larger quantities. Whenever the CPU must store a quantity in or read from **memory,** however, it can only deal in units as large as its **data bus** width, even if it has larger registers. The **data bus** is a pipeline to and from memory that enables the CPU to send pieces of information out and read them in. Only one device can use a bus at a time. Just as a larger diameter garden hose can move more water in a given time period, a wider data bus allows faster memory access. When we say that a processor is an 8-bit model, we generally mean that its data bus is 8 bits wide. By this standard, the Intel 8086 is a 16-bit chip, and its little brother, the 8088, which is used in the IBM PC, is actually an 8-bit chip, because its data bus is 8 bits wide.

Factors Affecting Performance

If a CPU has more registers, it is less dependent upon memory to perform many of its operations. Memory accesses are much slower than register accesses, therefore a chip that has more and/or larger registers will generally be faster. The 8086 and 8088 have exactly the same register set, even though their data buses are different. Another factor that determines **throughput,** or amount of work per unit of time, is the clock speed of the chip. In a microcomputer, all operations are synchronized by a very fast clock that ticks several million times per second. The same kind of chip might come in different clock speeds, with the faster speeds being more expensive because they are harder to produce.

In judging the power of the chip, it is also useful to look at how much memory it can handle. Memory looks to a CPU just like a series of mailboxes, each having a unique numeric **address.** Addresses are sent over an **address bus** to turn the proper memory locations on or off, and the largest address that is possible for a given CPU is directly determined by the width of its address bus. Most of the 8-bit processors had 16-bit address buses, which allowed them to access at most 65,536 (or 64K) **bytes** of data, because that is the largest number that can fit into 16 bits. Each bit of width added to the address bus multiplies the largest possible address figure by two.

Armed with these facts, we can talk intelligently about the relative merit of the Macintosh CPU versus other models. The Mac has as its core the **Motorola 68000CPU,** which is officially designated a 16-bit microprocessor. This implies that its data bus is 16 bits wide, twice as wide as the 6502, 8080, or 6800. Although the 68000 has the same data bus width as the 8086, it is a much more powerful chip, mostly because of its internal architecture, or what its registers look like. While the 8086/8088 each have eight 16-bit registers, the 68000 has **sixteen 32-bit registers.** The 68000 is designed so that all of its registers are **general-purpose,** and can be used for any operation. Intel's philosophy has been to assign registers to specific types of operations, meaning that the programmer must remember more information to program effectively with the 8086 or 8088 than with the 68000.

Another factor that affects programming ease is the way in which the processor divides up its memory space. The 8086 family divides memory up into **segments,** each of which can be 64K bytes long. If a larger data structure is required, it must be broken into segments, which can introduce additional design and programming time. The 68000 treats memory as one continuous string of addresses, to a maximum address of 16 megabytes. This is known as a linear address space. Many people that have used both systems prefer the latter for its simplicity.

Memory Usage

68000 clock speeds range from 6 Mhz to 12 Mhz, with the Macintosh using an 8 Mhz 68000. Faster CPUs require faster memory, which is considerably more expensive. The Macintosh uses sixteen 64K-bit RAMs to form its modifiable memory, amounting to 128K bytes. About 48K of this is used by the operating system, leaving a little over 80K for applications. This is rather small, especially since there are no slots to take add-on memory. Mac applications will tend to require less memory than similar applications on other machines, because the 64K ROM holds an extremely tight body of code, called the **User Interface ToolBox,** that applications may call to perform virtually any basic user interface operation (see chapter 16.)

The saving grace about the Mac's memory is that the 64K chips can be directly replaced by 256K memory chips when they become available, which should be in early 1985. Macs built after that time will include the larger complement, and some form of upgrade will probably be available through Apple dealers for older models. That will increase maximum capacity to 512K, or approximately that of a fully-loaded IBM PC. There's no such thing as enough RAM, but 512K should handle some pretty spectacular applications, because the Mac operating system code is so heavily trimmed and optimized for a small machine.

Having lots of registers available means that less memory operations are required, resulting in faster code. Macintosh OS and Lisa Pascal make extensive use of the 68000's powerful register set to speed up runtime execution speed. Of the sixteen registers available, 11 are used by the Pascal runtime code and QuickDraw in support of whatever application is running. This results in very good performance and space efficiency for Macintosh Pascal routines.

Access to the Toolbox

The 68000 has a **Trap** facility that is used extensively by the Mac operating system. A Trap is an instruction that causes the processor to interrupt whatever program is running and jump to some special code that is designed to service the trap. Traps can be caused by exception conditions, such as hardware failure or division by zero, or they can be intentionally generated by a program. In the latter case, the trap can be exploited as a very fast and easy method of transferring the processor's attention to a system routine, used to perform some commonly-needed function. The Macintosh uses 16-bit values as traps to transfer control to the ToolBox routines in the ROM, resulting in a considerable savings both in space and in execution speed for the application. The net effect is that the User Interface Toolbox becomes a logical extension of the instruction set of the 68000 itself.

QuickDraw

The chief reason for the Mac's designers choosing the 68000 chip was the fact that Bill Atkinson had already developed the extremely fast and powerful **QuickDraw** graphics package for the Lisa. This is not a program that the user ever sees, but rather a set of routines that other software calls to display various kinds of objects on the screen (see chapter 16.)

Quickdraw provided the Macintosh with a firm foundation on which to build the rest of the User Interface Toolbox, and also provided Lisa compatibility, a powerful incentive in itself.

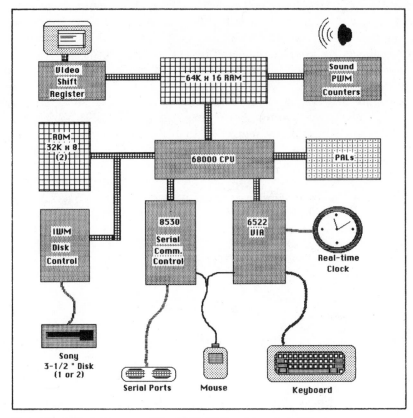

Figure 8.1   A Block Diagram of the 68000 CPU and Associated Devices.

An Efficient Hardware Design

68000-based implementations generally require a large number of chips to support the 68000 in its operation. One of Apple's goals was to minimize the number of physical chips on its boards, because this has a number of benefits, including increased reliability, easier manufacturing, lowered cost, less heat, and a smaller board size, permitting smaller overall package size. Chief Hardware Designer Burrell Smith, a one-time service technician who was discovered by Bill Atkinson during the Lisa project, applied himself to the task of reducing package count, inspired by the elegance of Steve Wozniak's original Apple II boards. Burrell made extensive use of **Programmable Array Logic (PAL) ICs** to incorporate the function of tens of smaller chips into single packages through painstaking and ingenious design work. The final package count of the Macintosh is less than that of the video controller card alone in the IBM PC, a testament to Burrell's and the entire design team's willingness to work unremittingly toward the most simple and elegant solution.

Another facet of this trend is the **IWM Disk Controller** chip, which integrates all hardware necessary to control the Sony 3½″ drives on a single chip. Apple engineers were so impressed with Wozniak's original controller design that they created the IWM, or Integrated Woz Machine, to replace the several packages that were found in the Apple II. This chip will be used by other Apple products as the standard controller.

The Macintosh uses a 6522 VIA to provide system timers, mouse support, general purpose I/O lines for video and sound flexibility, and for communication with the keyboard and battery-driven **real time clock.** A limited amount of RAM is designated **parameter RAM,** and holds settable system parameters under battery power when the machine is off. A Desk Accessory known as the **Control Panel** can be used to modify these parameters.

The last major part of the Mac's hardware core is the **Zilog 8530 SCC Serial Controller,** which provides communications support for the two **high-speed serial ports;** these we will describe in more detail in chapter 11. The SCC is capable of both **synchronous** and **asynchronous** communications at speeds of up to 230.4K bits per second, or 1 megabit per second with external clocking.

PROCESSOR:	MC68000, 32-bit architecture, 7.8336 MHz clock
MEMORY:	128K Bytes RAM, probable expansion to 512K 64K Bytes ROM holding User Interface Toolbox
DISK CAPACITY:	400K bytes per formatted disk, 3 1/2-inch diameter hard-shell media. One internal drive standard, external drive optional.
SCREEN:	4.75 by 7 inches (12 by 18 cm), P4 phosphor 512-pixel by 342-pixel bit-mapped display
INTERFACES:	Synchronous serial keyboard bus Two RS232/RS422 serial ports, 230.4K baud maximum (up to 0.920 megabit per second if clocked externally) Mouse interface External disk interface
SOUND GENERATOR:	4-voice sound with 8-bit digital-analog conversion using 22KHz sampling rate, 11Khz maximum frequency
INPUT:	Line voltage: 105 to 125 volts AC, RMS Frequency: 50 to 60 Hz Power: 60 watts
KEYBOARD:	58 key, 2-key rollover, software mapped. Optional numeric keypad
MOUSE:	Mechanical tracking, optical shaft encoding 3.54 pulse per mm (90 pulse per inch) of travel
CLOCK/CALENDAR:	CMOS custom chip with 4.5 volt (Eveready No. 523 or equivalent) user-replaceable battery backup

SIZE & WEIGHT:	Weight	Height	Width	Depth
Main Unit	7.5kg (16 lb, 8 oz.)	344 mm 13.5 inches	246 mm 9.7 inches	276 mm 10.9 inches
Keyboard	1.2 kg (2 lb, 8.5 oz.)	65 mm 2.6 inches	336 mm 13.2 inches	146 mm 5.8 inches
Mouse	.2 kg (7 oz.)	37 mm 1.5 inches	60 mm 2.4 inches	109 mm 4.3 inches

Figure 8.2 Summary of Hardware Specifications.

Eyes and Voice:
The Video and Sound Systems

The Amazing Bitmap

The Macintosh uses **bitmapped graphics** to achieve its video display of text and pictures. In this chapter we will explore what that means and what implications it has for the Mac's overall performance. We shall also look at the four-voice sound capability that is designed into the Mac, and how it is achieved.

Any computer system must devote a portion of its memory to the storage of information that is to be displayed on the screen. In many older computers and terminals without graphics capabilities, the screen is divided up into cells, one per character. Lines are typically 80 characters across, and there might be 24 or 25 lines, resulting in either 1920 or 2000 characters per screen. In the latter case, **2000 bytes** of memory would be allocated to the screen display, because it takes one byte to store the Ascii code for each character. The actual display is achieved by hardware; a chip called a **character generator** is constantly scanning that region of memory, and generating the proper commands to the video driver circuitry to place characters on the screen. Ultimately, the character generator must break up each character into a series of dots, and cause an electron gun in the CRT to place each dot in its proper place on the screen (see Figures 9-1 and 2.) The CPU is free to perform normal functions while this is happening, since the character generator is a totally separate device. The only limitation is that both chips cannot access memory at the same time unless **dual-ported RAM** is used, which essentially adds an extra bus from which to read and write memory.

There are several advantages to this approach: it is fast, requires relatively little memory, it's a well-established technique, and can be implemented on a single chip. The principal disadvantage is in flexibility: only characters can be drawn, and in the size and locations determined by the character generator. Crude graphics can sometimes be built from

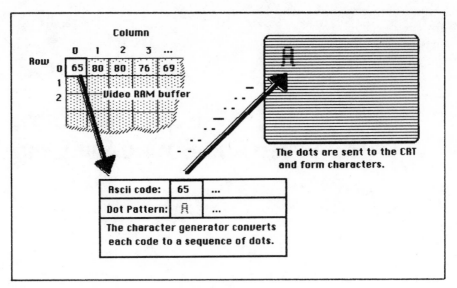

Figure 9.1 Video Using a Character Generator.

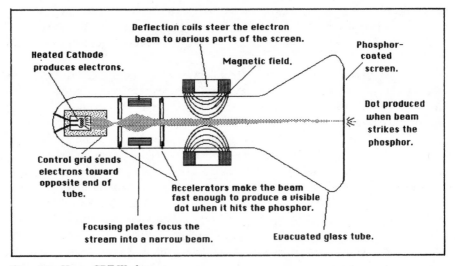

Figure 9.2 How a CRT Works.

characters, but this results in very poor resolution, and is useless for all but the simplest graphics. Unless the character generator is given its own totally separate section of memory or dual-ported RAM is used, the CPU must sit around and wait while the character generator uses the display memory known as **cycle-stealing.**

The windows, menus, icons and other features of the Macintosh desktop all require very high-resolution graphics to be feasible. This eliminated the character generator approach from practical consideration. Instead, Apple chose to implement a bitmapped display, which divides the screen into many tiny dots, and reserves a storage location in memory for each individual dot. Since each dot can only be on or off, it can be stored as a single bit with value 1 or 0. (see Figure 9-3.) The Macintosh screen has a

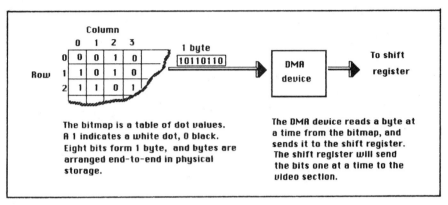

Figure 9.3   Video Using a Bitmap.

resolution of 512 dots horizontally and 342 dots vertically, resulting in a total of 175,104 dots that must be stored in memory. Since 8 bits form a byte, the Macintosh display memory occupies 21,888 **bytes** of RAM, or ten times as much memory as the character generator approach. But it allows software to have complete control over the display by writing values into memory that produce the desired bit patterns.

In a bitmapped display, software must determine the proper values to store into memory for text and graphics. This can cause a significant degradation in overall performance, because the CPU must devote its attention to this task instead of having the display managed by a dedicated chip. Bitmapped displays have not appeared in many 8-bit machines because there simply wasn't enough CPU power to manage the display along with normal operations. The power and speed of the 68000 make this approach possible in the Mac, but Apple still had to come up with some clever techniques to squeeze the most out of the processor's time.

In order to refresh the display fast enough to avoid visible flickering, dots must be sent to the screen very quickly (at the rate of 16 million per second in the Mac.) This is faster than the 68000 could move, even if it did nothing else. Special circuitry on the Mac performs **Direct Memory Access (DMA),** meaning that it accesses memory without going through the 68000. While this is happening, the 68000 can be performing an internal operation involving its registers, but it cannot access memory. The DMA section reads a 16-bit word of display memory data and sends it to a device known as a **shift register,** which picks off individual bits one at a time from the word and sends them to the video circuitry. While the bits are being sent to the video section, the 68000 can perform a memory access, and then the DMA device gets another word, and so on (see Figure 9-4.)

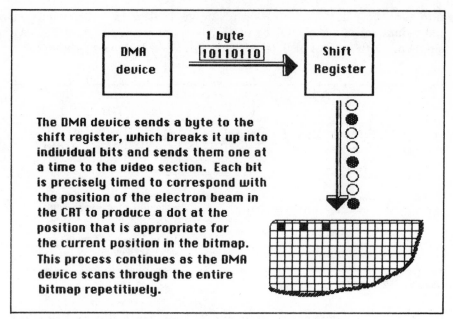

The DMA device sends a byte to the shift register, which breaks it up into individual bits and sends them one at a time to the video section. Each bit is precisely timed to correspond with the position of the electron beam in the CRT to produce a dot at the position that is appropriate for the current position in the bitmap. This process continues as the DMA device scans through the entire bitmap repetitively.

Figure 9.4   A Shift Register Sends Bits to the Video Section.

The two devices alternate memory accesses until the CRT performs a **horizontal retrace.** This occurs when the electron gun in the CRT has finished writing a line of dots to the screen, and moves over to the left side to start another line. During this period, the 68000 has full access to memory, and doesn't have to interleave with the DMA section. A small portion at the end of each line is devoted to reading a value and sending it to the sound generation circuit.

By interleaving in this manner, the Macintosh can support a high-resolution display with minimal hardware and not appreciably degrade performance. The technique also avoids **glitching,** a disturbance of the display that would occur if DMA and the CPU tried to access memory at the same time. Since accesses are mutually exclusive, glitching can never occur in the Macintosh.

The bitmap is physically stored by building bytes out of successive row bit values and laying them end-to-end. A row, which is 512 bits, occupies 64 bytes of memory, and there are 342 rows, yielding 21,888 bytes to store the entire screen (see Figure 9-5.) There are 72 dots to the inch on the physical Macintosh screen.

More About QuickDraw

Quickdraw is a collection of ROM routines that allow Macintosh applications to draw all of the impressive graphics structures that are a standard part of the user interface, such as windows, menus and dialog boxes. In addition, Quickdraw can form the basis for such applications as MacPaint

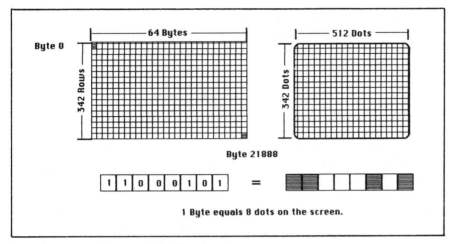

Figure 9.5   Physical Storage of the Bitmap.

and MacDraw (see Chapter 13) which are powerful graphics editors. Much of the hard work of generating graphics is done by Quickdraw under the control of the application.

QuickDraw enables programs to build images out of dots in the bitmap and perform various transformations on them, such as moving part of an image or rotating or scaling it. Quickdraw allows an arbitrary region of memory to be used as a bitmap, although one region is always set aside as storage for the whole screen. Programs can define their own **regions** in which to build images, and then switch regions to provide animation or to build images for printing.

A program sets up its drawing environment with QuickDraw by defining what is known as a **GrafPort.** A GrafPort associates a bit image in memory with a **coordinate system** that assigns each bit a numeric location relative to an origin. Several GrafPorts can use the same bit image, and define several different coordinate systems for use with the bit image. Once a drawing has been created in a given coordinate system, that drawing can be moved on the screen by simply moving the origin of the coordinate system relative to the physical bit image. This can be accomplished with a single call to QuickDraw, and should afford an inkling of why QuickDraw is so powerful.

A **pattern** is defined within QuickDraw as an 8-bit by 8-bit rectangle, to be repeated by putting successive rectangles next to each other. A region of a drawing can be filled with any pattern that is definable in this manner. Various shades of halftone gray as well as more distinctive patterns are provided in the MacPaint program, and there is a facility for creating your own pattern by turning individual dots on or off within an 8-by-8 rectangle (see Chapter 13.)

Making QuickDraw Fit

All of the Macintosh Toolbox routines use QuickDraw to place images on the screen. We have only had room here to cover a small fraction of the powerful features that QuickDraw provides. The Macintosh software environment would have been an impossible dream were it not for the ingenuity of Bill Atkinson in compressing the QuickDraw code into a little over 20K of assembly language for the Mac ROM. When originally developed for the Lisa as a Pascal prototype, QuickDraw occupied around 160K, nearly as much as the entire memory complement of the Mac. Chapter 16 will describe in more detail the programming interface to the QuickDraw package.

Amazing Sounds

At its unveiling on January 24, 1984, the Macintosh was given the podium to introduce itself. It did so in grand style, not only rolling a large-font version of its name across the screen and doing animated drawings, but **speaking** four or five sentences! This demonstration clearly showed the great flexibility of the Mac's four-voice sound synthesis hardware and software.

This flexibility is achieved by providing a very general, and fairly fast, hardware capability for producing sound, and making it do specific things with software. The Macintosh is able to produce sounds by using a technique known as **digital-to-analog conversion.** To understand this concept, let's first look at the physics of sound.

We hear sounds when a physical event sets up a **vibratory motion** in a **medium** such as air or water. When something vibrates back and forth, its motion is transmitted to the molecules of air or other medium in contact with it, and they in turn transmit their motion to their neighbors, and so on. Eventually, the motion is transmitted to our eardrum, at which point we hear a sound. If you examined the motion of a drum head that someone had hit, and compared it to the motion of their eardrums, you would find that the two exhibited very similar motions, except that the eardrum doesn't have as far to move as the drum head. This phenomenon is known as **sympathetic vibration,** and requires a medium of some sort to occur. That's why no sound can occur in a vacuum.

If we graphed the positions of the drum head and the eardrums over time, we would see something like Figure 9-6. At first, the drum head moves farthest, and the sound is loudest. It then bounces back to the other side, losing a little momentum in the process, and this continues until the motion dies out. The degree to which the head has traveled away from its normal position is called the **amplitude** of its motion. The amplitude directly corresponds to the **volume,** or amplitude, of the sound that it makes. The path that the graph of the head's position describes is called its **waveform,** and is a mathematical representation of the actual sound.

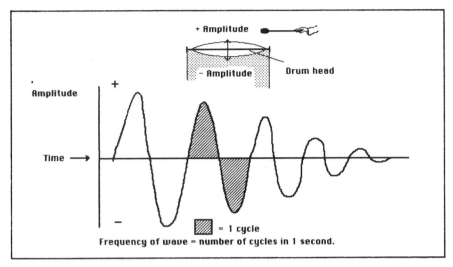

Figure 9.6   Waveform of A Percussive Sound.

Representing Sound as Numbers

Computers can only represent things internally as numbers. Using numbers, they can represent just about any other form of information, including sounds. The graph of the drum's waveform is very smooth, because its amplitude is continuously varying. In order to represent the waveform inside of a computer, it's necessary to chop the time axis up into slices, and decide upon a suitable number to represent the amplitude of the wave for each slice (see Figure 9-7.) Each of these numbers can then be stored as a byte in memory representing the amplitude at a certain point in time.

In addition to amplitude, or volume, we also discriminate sounds by their pitch. The technical term for pitch is **frequency;** in physical terms, frequency corresponds to how rapidly the object is vibrating, or how often its amplitude crosses the zero point in a **unit of time.** If we take a piece of the waveform, and only look at a section composed of a high peak followed by a valley, that is called a **cycle.** Frequency is expressed in cycles **per second,** or **Hertz;** middle A on a piano is 440 Hertz, and is neither very high nor very low. Humans can generally hear well up to around 10,000 Hertz; higher sounds become very difficult to discriminate.

In order to create a sound on the Macintosh, it is necessary to set up a list of numbers that correspond to amplitudes of the proposed sound at regular time intervals, and which together comprise a single cycle of the wave. This is known as a **waveform table.** The Mac operating system will repeatedly scan this waveform table at a rate set by the caller, and turn the amplitude values into motions of the speaker cone. This is performed by a device known as a digital-to-analog converter, which transforms the number value into a **voltage** that will cause the speaker cone to move a certain distance, and thereby produce a sound.

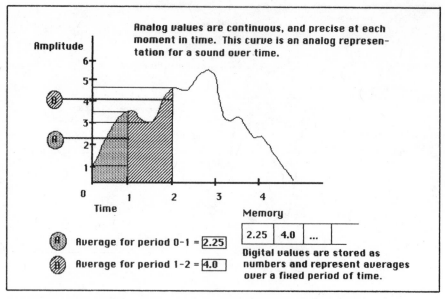

Figure 9.7 Analog and Digital Representations of Audio Information.

Up to four waveform tables can be used at one time, allowing up to four **voices,** or separate tones, to be heard simultaneously. If four voices are used, the 68000 must spend 50% of its time loading the proper sound values into the sound buffer, which would significantly slow the rest of an application.

Advantages

Building a waveform table in memory provides an immense degree of flexibility in the Mac's sound system. The IBM PC is capable of only single-voice sound, and the **timbre,** or quality, of the sound cannot be modified. Timbre is the characteristic that separates a flute from a violin, even when they are playing at the same frequency and amplitude. Timbre can only be created by building the waveform from individual values in a table such as the Macintosh utilizes. As is the case in other parts of the Mac's programming environment, other systems might be easier, but the Mac is much more powerful than any of the other machines in its price category relative to sound generation. The power of the 6800 and a clever scheme were required for this capability to be provided without robbing more than 50% of the CPU's time.

I am looking to third-party vendors to provide some really incredible sound generation/synthesis software for the Macintosh. An external speaker jack is provided, enabling you to plug the Macintosh into your stereo rather than be limited by the Mac's 3-watt speaker. This is going to be a fun area to watch as programmers discover the immense capabilities of Macintosh sound.

10

The Mouse and Keyboard

The Macintosh uses both a **mouse** and a **keyboard** to accept input from the user. The mouse is a small box that sits on your desk, fits easily into your hand, and has a single button on the top (see Figure 10-1.) Mechanically, this mouse is very similar to the one used on the Lisa, but their external appearance is somewhat different. Apple plans eventually to use identical mice on all of their systems, and these will look very close to the Macintosh model.

Mouse Anatomy

Inside the mouse, there is a steel ball covered with rubber which contacts the surface upon which the mouse is placed (see Figure 10-2.) This ball rolls as the mouse is moved across a surface, and it turns two rollers that sit at right angles to each other. One roller controls the horizontal position of the pointer on the screen, and one the vertical. A third roller is spring-loaded, and keeps the ball in contact with the other two. The rollers transmit signals over the mouse's cord that tell the mouse input hardware how far it has moved in each direction.

The mouse hardware is constantly keeping track of the mouse's position, and this information is available to Mac software whenever it is needed. When you depress the button on the mouse, the operating system **posts an event,** which is a way of telling the application that something has happened that it should check on.

The mouse is a little strange to use at first, and you will find that you have some difficulty pointing with a lot of accuracy. Some practice is necessary before you can comfortably associate movements of your hand with the position of the pointer. A demonstration and training program that comes with the Mac provides an excellent chance to practice mouse skills. After a couple of hours, it becomes quite natural, and is much easier to use than the keyboard for many purposes. The only time that you have to use the keyboard for anything on the Mac is entering text, and that seems to come up a lot less than on other machines.

Figure 10.1 Macintosh and its Mouse

One common complaint about the mouse in general is that it requires a lot of desk space to use. I have found that my ability to use the mouse in a smaller area has been directly proportional to how long I have had it. At this point, I can use a mouse comfortably in an area not much wider than the mouse itself, because I have gotten very good at picking it up several times to move it across the screen. This essentially defuses the not-enough-room argument for me.

Problems

The mouse isn't ideal for everything. For drawing, especially freehand drawing and painting, the mouse seems rather clumsy. It wouldn't surprise me if a vendor came up with a tablet interface for the Mac's serial port that could be used with MacPaint and MacDraw. On the whole, though, the mouse is a good solution to many user interface problems.

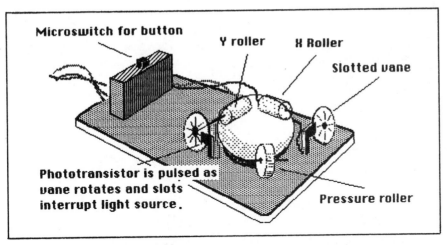

Figure 10.2   Inside the Macintosh Mouse.

One difficulty with the mouse is that, after several days of use, it tends to accumulate dirt on the rollers that eventually causes it to slip. At first I thought I had a defective mouse, and it was really quite infuriating to use. Then I tried scraping the dirt from the rollers with a small screwdriver, which restored the mouse to normality. If you ever notice the mouse slipping appreciably, follow the directions to remove the ball, and in addition to checking the ball for dirt, see if there is a small band of dirt around the rollers. If so, scrape them gently and remove the residue from the inside of the cavity before you replace the ball, or it will be back in no time. It helps to frequently clean the area of your desk that the mouse is in with a damp cloth.

Other than that small problem, I have never had anything go wrong with the mouse. It's well built, and it really seems to be quite sturdy. An adjustment in the Control Panel desk accessory enables you to adjust the rate at which the cursor moves with respect to the mouse. There is a high speed and a low speed, the latter being useful for exacting work such as in MacPaint.

The Keyboard

The Macintosh keyboard is very much like a typewriter keyboard (see photo.) You touch typists out there would be quite comfortable on this keyboard (as opposed to the IBM PC and PC/Jr keyboards.) The feel is firm, not spongy, and there is a solidity to the keys that I like very much. I actually prefer the firmness of the Mac's keyboard to the Lisa's, which tends to be a little sloppy.

Because of the mouse, very few extra keys are present to confuse the first time user. There is an "Option" key, that provides access to a character graphics set and some esoteric options in applications, and a "Command" key with a design on it that allows you to substitute a keystroke for moving the mouse and selecting certain menu options. For instance, you can press "Command" and "C" simultaneously instead of selecting **Copy** in the **Edit** menu. I now use these "expert" commands almost exclusively rather than their somewhat time-consuming mouse equivalents. The beauty is that you don't have to remember all sorts of bizarre control-key combinations to perform any given operation on the Mac.

The Mac keyboard is 13″ by 5½″, much smaller than the Lisa's or the IBM's (18″ by 7½″). It helps not to have a lot of special-purpose keys around. There is a **Desk Accessory** called **Key Caps,** covered more extensively in chapter 7, that can be used to see the graphics characters that are available (see Figure 10-3.)

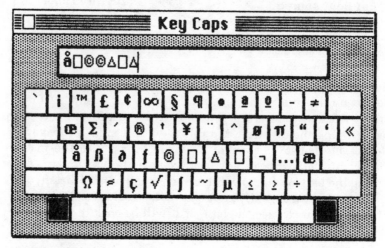

Figure 10.3   Graphics Characters Available on the Macintosh Keyboard.

The keyboard has its own microprocessor, and communicates with the main unit over a four-wire synchronous serial interface. This means that the keys that you type are converted into streams of pulses that are sent to the main unit in lock step with a high-speed clock. The keyboard is capable of **2-key rollover,** meaning that it knows if you have hit two keys simultaneously, but not any more than two. The cable has the same connectors as a telephone handset cord, and in fact you could probably substitute one for the other if things got tough, or you wanted to type while sitting in the next room.

Like the mouse, the information that comes in from the keyboard is tracked and stored by the operating system. Even if you type faster than an application can keep up with, the operating system holds those keys in a **queue,** or ordered list, until the application is ready to handle them. This is known as the **event queue,** and informs applications of all significant external events, including activity from the mouse, keyboard and disks, in the order that they occurred.

Mac and Lisa Compatibility

A nice touch is that the Lisa and Macintosh keyboards have exactly the **same layout,** so that you can move between the two very easily. Since the Lisa II can run Mac software, there will be a significant number of people who use both; for instance, you might have a Mac at home and a Lisa in the office. Keyboard compatibility will be highly appreciated by that group. There is also an **external numeric keypad** available from Apple for the Mac that is exactly the same as the Lisa numeric keypad. It arranges the numbers in a calculator format for more efficient entry of rows of numeric data. This plugs into the main keyboard, which in turn plugs into the Mac.

11

Disks, Printers and Communications

Disk drives are the part of a computer system that allow permanent storage of information when the machine is turned off. There are several different parts to a typical disk storage system (see Figure 11-1.) The physi-

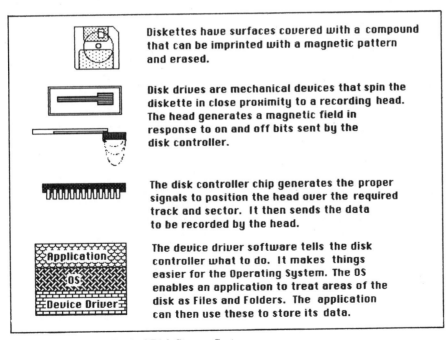

Diskettes have surfaces covered with a compound that can be imprinted with a magnetic pattern and erased.

Disk drives are mechanical devices that spin the diskette in close proximity to a recording head. The head generates a magnetic field in response to on and off bits sent by the disk controller.

The disk controller chip generates the proper signals to position the head over the required track and sector. It then sends the data to be recorded by the head.

The device driver software tells the disk controller what to do. It makes things easier for the Operating System. The OS enables an application to treat areas of the disk as Files and Folders. The application can then use these to store its data.

Figure 11.1 Parts of a Typical Disk Storage System.

cal disks, called the **media,** have surfaces covered with a magnetic material capable of holding patterns of information. These come in a variety of styles and sizes, from 3¼″ up to 8″ in diameter. The **drives** are mechanical devices that have **heads,** similar in function to the heads on a tape deck. A hub grips the center of the diskette, and spins it at several hundred revolutions per minute while the heads ride very close to the surface of the diskette, not actually touching it. Magnetic fields are created by the heads in patterns corresponding to the data that is sent to them, and they magnetically imprint these patterns on the surface of the disk.

The drive itself is a mechanical device, not capable in its own right of doing anything but turning the diskettes and moving its heads. The **disk controller** is an electronic device that tells the drive what to do by way of electrical signals. It is the controller that enables the drives to record and playback digital data in a way that is useful for computers. Often disk controllers and drives are made by different manufacturers and later integrated into a computer system. The disk controller for the Mac is a custom Apple chip, the **IWM,** that incorporates the Apple II's controller hardware in a single package.

A disk controller, in turn, is controlled by software in the operating system called a **device manager.** This is software that is designed specifically for a certain controller and drive. Controlling the device manager is more sophisticated software that handles a lot of the housekeeping chores necessary to keep track of what data is stored on the disk and where. This software is known on the Macintosh as the **File Manager.** Many kinds of disk devices can be used with the Mac file manager because it has been designed so that device differences are relevant only to the device managers. They translate between the specific commands used by the device and the more general scheme used by the file manager. This will make it relatively easy for other vendors to supply hard disks and other models of floppy disks for the Mac; they need only build the hardware interface and the proper device driver.

Two different systems may not be able to trade disks even though they use exactly the same type of drives, media and controllers. That's because the software **formats** the disk in a certain way by recording marker areas on the disk that divide it up into sections. Even different versions of the same operating system might use different formats, as was the case when the Apple II went from 13 sector format to 16 sector format with the release of DOS 3.3. Let's look at some general principles of how disks are divided up by software formatting.

Figure 11-2 shows the circular disk divided up into two different kinds of physical grouping. First, the disk is broken into concentric circular bands called **tracks.** These are distinguished by their distance from the center of the disk. Secondly, each track is divided into regions called **sectors.** As you can see, the tracks near the outer edge of the disk are longer, and therefore could theoretically contain more sectors. Once formatted, a disk contains recorded markers that tell where each sector starts and ends on each track.

When the Macintosh was first designed, it used the same 5¼″ diskettes as the Lisa I. Midway through the project, Apple became interested in some new drives that Sony had developed, which used "micro-floppy" 3½″ disks housed in a rigid plastic container. Because the disk itself was stiffer and moved less, and was therefore less prone to error, the disk could be formatted with more tracks and sectors than a standard floppy disk. When the Mac designers were able to assure themselves that these drives could be produced reliably and in quantity, they changed the design to fit the new drives.

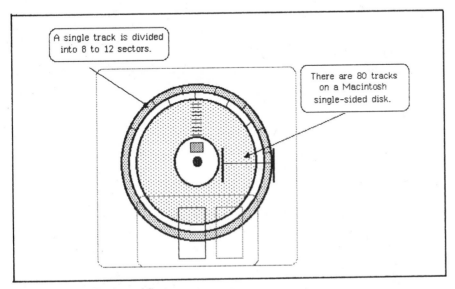

Figure 11.2 Disk Tracks and Sectors.

Sony had to make two custom changes, however, before the drives would be acceptable for the Macintosh. On most disk drives, to eject the disk you lift a door or press a button, and the hardware ejects the disk regardless of what the software is doing. This can result in loss of data if you happen to fling the door open when the computer is in the middle of writing something important to the disk. The Lisa's 5¼″ drives were built in such a way that the disks would only be ejected after the operating system had finished writing the necessary information out to disk to ensure that it was up to date. The buttons on the Lisa drives are only signals to the operating system that you want an eject, as opposed to mechanical buttons that can actually release the disk.

The Mac team wanted this same protection in the Sony drives, so Sony had to go back to the drawing board to provide this feature. The other modification was that Apple had developed a method of varying the rotation speed of the disk that resulted in more reliable transfers and higher density storage for the Lisa I. Most disks turn at a constant rate. If you have ever watched a spinning phonograph record, you might have noticed that the outer grooves move much faster than the inner ones. This results in less information per linear unit being recorded in the outer grooves as compared to the inner ones.

If you were to vary the speed of the record so that all of the grooves move at the same rate with respect to the playback cartridge, you would have both longer records and a much more complex and expensive turntable. You would have to turn the record slower when the cartridge was over the outer grooves, and gradually speed up as it moved in. Apple applied this technology to disks, yielding a significant increase in storage per disk. For instance, the Macintosh is able to store 400K bytes on a single-sided Sony disk, while other machines that use constant-speed drives can only store 270K. That's about a 50% improvement. Part of this is also due to the fact that Sony modified the drives, at Apple's behest, to read and write 80 tracks instead of the normal 70.

The Mac operating system allocates storage on the Sony disks in **blocks.** A block is a region of the disk, possibly containing several sectors; all blocks on a disk are the same size, 512 bytes on the Sony disks. The disk as a whole is assigned a **volume,** which is really just a logical description of the disk to the operating system. The volume gives a name to the disk and holds information about all of the files stored on it. Each block has two parts: a **tag** and a **data area.** The tag is very important, because it contains information about the file that the block belongs to so that the file can be reconstructed in case of partial damage to the disk. This is a safety measure that costs some storage, but is probably worth it in reliability. The data area of the block is the only part that can be read or written by applications.

After the Sony disk is formatted, it contains two **boot blocks** and a **master directory block.** These blocks are always placed in the same physical location on the disk; the boot blocks contain information necessary for starting the system up when Mac is turned on. The master directory block contains the volume name, the date and time when it was last **backed up,** (or copied), and other essential data for the volume. It also shows how the blocks on the volume are grouped together to form **files,** which are named collections of data that can be documents, applications or a variety of other things.

Apple uses the Sony drives on both the Mac and the Lisa 2, and disks may be exchanged between the two. Most Lisa applications won't run on the Mac because of memory size, but most Mac applications should work on the Lisa. When Sony is able to make the drives in quantity with two heads instead of one, these disks will store **800K bytes** of data instead of 400K.

After using the Sony disks for awhile, conventional 5¼″ floppy disks seem crude and primitive. The Sony disks can be thrown in the mail, fit in your pocket, and could probably reside there for some time without being damaged, because a metal door protects the actual disk surface. They feel very substantial, and have a write-protect button that slides back and forth instead of using sticky little tags that you have to peel off. The drives are very quiet in operation. A motor ejects the disk, a somewhat disconcerting experience the first time around. There is no button or door to eject the disk anywhere on the machine; the only way to accomplish an eject is to make a menu or dialog selection.

I would say on the basis of my experience with these disks that the days are numbered for the old formats. The only drawback to the Sonys right now is that they aren't on a lot of machines, but that's changing rapidly (at the rate of one Mac every 27 seconds) other manfacturers have come out with small-format drives, but the Apple 32 line should present a commanding argument for Sony's de facto acceptance.

A major problem that I have observed with the Mac's disk drive is that it's singular, not plural. Of course, that would add to price and weight, which is why there is only one in the basic package. But with one drive that holds 400K you will find yourself doing a lot of disk swapping. It would seem that the Finder could make use of some application memory to do its copying in larger chunks, but that wasn't a feature of the disks that I've been working with.

Functionally, copying between disks is relatively straightforward once you do it a couple of times. You have to select the disk window, eject the disk, put in the new one, and drag any files that you want to copy to the other disk. Thereafter, you will be prompted to insert the original disk whenever you want to do something substantial on the new one, because the Finder apparently needs to use its files on the original disk for support. This can be a little disconcerting. I would hope that Apple makes this area a little less confusing with future releases, but a lot of it is a necessary evil of single-drive systems. When and if they go to 800K drives, there will be much less need to use multiple disks. For now, I would strongly consider going the extra money for an external drive, particularly if you are going to be using large files, editing a lot of text, and so on.

Possible bright spots are Tecmar's and Davong's external hard disks, which were announced but unreleased at the time of this writing. These units will plug into one of the high-speed serial connectors, and otherwise look like a normal, albeit large, drive to the Finder. Depending on their pricing strategy and the performance of the unit, hard disks could be a real boon to Macintosh owners. I went to an IBM PC/XT after using a diskette-based PC for about a year, and the difference in functional simplicity due to never worrying about which disk a file is on is enormous. Apple plans to develop a hard disk as well, and I expect that by early 1985 there will be a number of products in this area.

Now, let's talk a bit about communications. The ability to exchange information electronically via computer is more and more becoming an essential item, both in the business world and at home. The range of activities that can be carried out with a computer over the phone lines is increasing geometrically, and is already overwhelming in its diversity. One need only browse through an index to dialup services like **Compuserve** or **The Source** to see a mind-boggling array of resources available to those who have the technology to use them. A small sample includes electronic banking, electronic mail, commodity news, Standard and Poor's information, online clubs and special interest groups, flight planning, and thousands more.

Another aspect to computer communications is local area networking, which allows many computers in close proximity to be linked together so that they can share data or use common peripherals like printers or large-capacity hard disks. This is becoming increasingly desirable as personal computers proliferate in the offices of more and more employees, and computer budgets expand at a noteworthy rate.

While these two areas impose very different hardware requirements, today's computers must be capable of supporting both to be really effective. Communication via phone lines requires that the machine support the standard **RS-232 electrical interface,** which is rather old and slow, but is the means by which almost all personal computers and communications devices talk to each other. Local area networks, on the other hand, require a very high data rate and some degree of compatibility with other equipment, although very little has occurred in the area of standardization.

In a typical communications system, the personal computer cannot put data on the phone lines directly; it must use a device called a **modem** which translates data from electrical signals into tones that can be carried over standard telephone lines. The computer communicates with the modem by means of a **serial interface.** This is necessary because various computers have a variety of different internal hardware for manipulating data, and most of them are incompatible. Inside, they use a **parallel** representation for data. This means that if a word, or 16 bits, of data is moved from one place to another, the entire word is picked up and moved, all 16 bits in parallel. The computer has a bus with 16 lines on it, one for each of the bits. Manufacturers have many different specifications for these buses, involving timing, voltage levels and other factors. There is a real Tower of Babel situation as far as connecting them together is concerned.

To address this problem, the Electronic Industries Association came up with what is known as the RS-232 serial interface specification many years ago as a way for all systems to use a common hardware method for communications. RS-232 is principally an electrical specification that sets certain voltages and load limits, but it was intended for a certain software method of sending and receiving data called **serialization.** To serialize means to string out in a series of pieces over time—in this case, the bits are sent, one by one, as specific voltage levels on lines of a 25-conductor cable.

Most modems and many printers use RS-232 as the standard means of communicating with a computer. There are several compatibility issues that must be resolved before two devices can communicate serially. One is how many bits each byte of data will be "packaged" in when it is sent over the line. Another is speed, or how many bits per second are to be sent. There are several standard speeds at which RS-232 serial communications are carried out, ranging up to 19,200 bits per second. When the standard was designed, this was considered quite fast; today, however, RS-232 is much too slow to support communications tasks that require moving a lot of data very quickly, such as local-area networks.

An RS-232 cable is also limited to around 100 feet for reliable communications at the highest speed; any longer than that, and errors begin occurring. The problem is that the RS-232 lines use a common ground wire, and at high speeds over long distances, signals begin to cross over from one wire to the others, a condition known as **crosstalk.** To remove these drawbacks, the EIA recently drew up another standard, called **RS-422,** that would improve upon RS-232 by supporting higher speeds over longer distances.

The chief improvement in the RS-422 specification is that it requires **balanced lines** for each of the signals. This means that, instead of each signal having one wire and sharing a common ground with the others, there are two wires for each signal, having voltages that are equal in magnitude but opposite in polarity. This tends to cancel out any interference that is picked up by the cable along its path, and allows much longer runs as well as higher speeds.

The difficulty is that very few hardware vendors support RS-422 yet, partially because so much of the world has a huge investment in RS-232 equipment. Apple's approach with the Macintosh was to support both, with the protocol being determined by software rather than hardware. This allows you to plug a standard RS-232 cable into your modem and the Mac and use it to dial up Compuserve, and at the same time be able to use the high-speed capability of the other port for linking with other Macs or peripherals. Both protocols can utilize the same physical connector type, known as DB-9 because it requires 9 pins. Apple chose the powerful **Zilog 8530 Serial Communications Controller** to manage the serial ports. It is capable of up to one million bits per second transfer rate, which is fast enough to be able to use the serial ports for add-on disk drives or local-area networks.

Because the Mac was designed for mass production, no hardware flexibility was permitted in the main cabinet; there are no **slots** as there are in the Apple II to add other peripherals or more memory. Instead, the Mac provides very high-performance serial ports as a means of adding peripherals. This made RS-422 a necessity, because the old standard was simply too slow. Apple has a concept called **"virtual slots"** that allows peripherals to be chained together on a common cable from a single RS-422 port, and each of them will be treated as though it resided in a distinct and unique hardware location. This provides virtually limitless expandability, and is an example of the kind of innovative design work that characterizes the whole of the Macintosh.

To support this scheme, each peripheral, whether it is a disk, printer, or other device, will have to have its own microprocessor and be somewhat "intelligent". This is the trend in peripherals anyway, because a microprocessor can now be added to a design for very little cost, and there is a lot of benefit to having a "smart" device that can respond more flexibly to the situations that confront it. So Apple's choice would seem to be a very timely and clever one; the true story on that will be told by the vendors that are developing external hardware.

Apple is working on a scheme for interconnection called **Applebus** that will exploit the high-speed serial ports and enable Macs and Lisa IIs to share peripherals. This will enhance the utility of the entire Apple 32 line, since it will allow work stations to be suited to the individuals who need to use them, sharing the expensive hardware like large-capacity hard disks. Apple also has plans for a 72 Megabyte hard disk that would attach to a Lisa II and could act as a common disk for all stations on the network.

Applebus utilizes **twisted pairs** of wires that are connected to each Mac or Lisa via a box that has a single RS-422 cable and two twisted pair connections. The maximum length for the twisted pairs for the entire network is 1000 feet and transmission occurs at a speed of 230.4K bits per second. The pairs are transformer-isolated from the RS-422 connection, providing noise immunity. Up to 32 stations can be connected to a given Applebus network, and these can be either Lisa IIs or Macs. The communications protocol used on Applebus will be SDLC, which is a bit-oriented, synchronous full-duplex protocol developed by IBM. If you don't know what those terms mean, you can look them up in a communications text; for now, suffice it to say that Apple has IBM compatibility in mind in their design for Applebus.

Apple has publicly expressed a commitment to support IBM's Local Area Network for the PC when it is announced, and Apple's choice of SDLC will no doubt poise them well for that task. Nobody knows what exactly IBM's network will be, but SDLC is a pretty good bet. At worst, a conversion device will be necessary to go between the two LANs. It will probably be up to third-party software houses to provide the software to support the interconnection of Apple 32 machines with IBM PCs.

The idea of sharing peripherals is nice, but doesn't really deserve to be called a "network" in the true sense of the term. A true network would allow people to have access to the files on any other workstation (if they weren't protected), and even run applications on other stations if theirs was overloaded. We're a long way from that today, but Apple is paving the way for a genuine network with the Apple 32 line's powerful processors, high-speed communications and desktop software. There is already a lot of industry interest in the communications potential of the Mac and Lisa, but it will take some time for developers to explore the new technology.

Apple is taking a very aggressive role in encouraging developers to produce hardware and software that will make Applebus into an electronic mail system and a sophisticated network in the true sense of the term. They view Applebus, like the Mac, as providing a **vehicle** that can be creatively exploited by the top minds of the industry. Apple itself is only committing to providing the groundwork, which is wiser than making a lot of promises that they can't deliver. Exactly how Applebus will look a year from now depends largely upon the initiative of the developers; judging from the amount of interest already generated, some very substantial communications products should be seen from companies like Davong and Tecmar for the Macintosh.

Apple has also developed a "protocol converter" box, called **AppleLine,** that will provide **IBM 3278 compatibility** for Macs and Lisa IIs, thereby mating the Apple 32 line with the world of IBM mainframes and minicomputers. This is a very large market, particularly in the Fortune 500 arena. Software support in **MacTerminal** will allow the Mac to emulate, or look like, an IBM 3278-2 terminal, which is commonly used with IBM mainframes. 3278 compatibility should prove appealing to companies who recognize the need for personal workstations, but have a large investment in mainframe technology. Appleline converts from the RS-422 cable to a coaxial cable that can be directly connected to IBM 3274-type cluster controllers.

For companies that don't have a 3274, but are interested in the idea of 3278 emulation with Lisas and Macs, Apple has developed the **Apple Cluster Controller,** providing 3274 emulation for from 3 to 7 Apple 32 machines. This is a "black box" that performs the same operations as the much more expensive 3274 would, supporting coaxial links to the Macs and Lisas.

An external **300/1200 baud modem** is available from Apple that plugs into the serial port, and the **MacTerminal** application allows the Mac to act like a DEC VT100 or VT52 terminal and use dialup communications services (MacTerminal will be covered in Chapter 14.) The Apple Modem is compatible with US Robotics' Passport, and both share a similar command set with the Hayes Smartmodems. There are enough differences, however, that communications software designed specifically for Hayes has a good chance of not working with the Apple modem.

An important feature of the Mac's internal design is **concurrent I/O (input/output) processing.** When the Mac is receiving data over the serial ports, it can also be accessing the disk, or the 68000 CPU can be doing other non-I/O computation. In most personal computer systems, every time a disk access is made, the entire system has to wait for the motor to come up to speed, which could take almost a second. This is enough time for the processor to handle hundreds of thousands of instructions, and it is just wasted.

The reason that concurrent I/O is possible is through a combination of **interrupt-driven architecture** and clever programming. Interrupts provide a mechanism by which other hardware can function independently of the 68000, but notify it (interrupt it) when an important event has occurred, such as the disk motor coming up to speed. The 68000 then performs whatever operations are appropriate for that interrupt via an **interrupt handler,** and returns to its normal operations. When the CPU services the interrupt, its entire environment is saved so that it can return to it later as though nothing had happened.

The clever programming comes in when it is necessary to do both disk operations and high-speed serial communications simultaneously. If the processor was a little slow in responding to an interrupt, data could be lost from the serial port, because it can come in extremely fast. So the disk code checks after writing every two bytes to see if there is any data coming in on the serial port, and if so, retrieves it and stores it in memory. This will prove very useful if the Mac needs to receive a file over the serial line and write it out to disk simultaneously, without slowing down the communications line. Requirements like this are common in communications networks; one example is systems that broadcast a continuous stream of financial data that must be captured or lost, such as floor data from a financial exchange.

To sum up, the communications capability of the Macintosh is very attractive in relation to its current competition, not only because of the dual support for RS232/RS422, and mainframe compatability, but also the internal interrupt structure that makes concurrent I/O at high speeds possible.

The **Imagewriter** dot-matrix printer allows you to print both text and graphics. It connects to one of the two serial ports, and is rated at 160 characters per second. The Macintosh can use two different methods to print via the Imagewriter. In **graphics mode,** the printer operates in a manner analogous to the display screen of the Mac, placing dots on the page at positions specified by the printer driver code. The print head of the Imagewriter is an array of **pins** which can be individually projected to make dots on paper (see Figure 11-3.) Since there are eight pins in a vertical

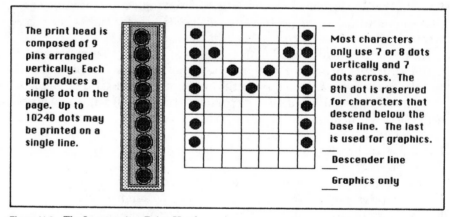

The print head is composed of 9 pins arranged vertically. Each pin produces a single dot on the page. Up to 10240 dots may be printed on a single line.

Most characters only use 7 or 8 dots vertically and 7 dots across. The 8th dot is reserved for characters that descend below the base line. The last is used for graphics.

Descender line

Graphics only

Figure 11.3 The Imagewriter Print Head.

column, a byte of data can be used to specify which dots are to be printed for a single column of graphics data. A bit with the value 1 indicates a dot, and a 0 leaves that dot blank.

To print a picture created on the Mac, or a direct image of the screen, the operating system divides up the graphics image into bands that are 8 bits tall. These are then encoded into successive columns, and sent column by column to the Imagewriter. The result is a very close image of what is displayed on the screen. Many of the figures in this book were produced in MacPaint and printed via that application. The Mac screen can also be printed at any time by pressing the Command, Shift, and 4 keys down with Caps Lock on. This will dump an exact image of the screen to the printer, which is a boon for documentation.

The fonts that are available in many of the Mac applications can be printed on the Imagewriter by sending a direct graphics image of the dots on the screen, but this isn't very fast. In **draft mode,** the print software sends a **character code** for each character of text rather than its graphic image. The printer has its own **character generator,** and can create the correct pattern of dots from the character code. This is the only way to print text at the Imagewriter's top speed of **160 characters per second,** but the font is restricted to the one stored in the printer's character generator ROM. This is fine for quick drafts, in which appearances are less important than content. For high-quality text, or to print combined text and graphics, either **high-resolution** or **low-resolution graphics mode** must be used. Low-res mode is faster, because there are less dots per square inch to be sent and printed. Figure 11-4 shows some examples of text and graphics printed in the various modes.

This is high-quality print mode. It uses the high-resolution graphics setting of the Imagewriter printer.

This is standard print mode. It uses the low-resolution graphics setting of the Imagewriter printer.

This is draft print mode. It uses the native character set of the Imagewriter printer, and cannot print Macintosh graphics.

Figure 11.4 High-Quality, Standard and Draft Modes.

From a programming point of view, using the printer to print graphics images is relatively easy. Images are still created via QuickDraw, and different output routines are linked in to drive the printer instead of the screen. This provides a lot of independence between the application and the output methodology, and is an example of the clean, modular approach that was used throughout the design of the operating system. The printer routines provide hooks for defining new types of printers, ensuring easy update when third-party vendors provide output devices for the Mac.

An interesting feature of printing on both the Mac and the Lisa is the ability to turn an image on its side, and print it lengthwise on the printer! This provides for drawings that are longer or wider than a standard sheet of paper.

Apple also has plans for a **laser printer** that would attach to the serial ports of either the Lisa or the Mac, and cost less than $4000. This type of device provides noiseless, fast, extremely high resolution hardcopy. A laser printer could provide near-typeset quality document printing for Macs and

Lisas, and be shared by up to 32 work stations on the AppleBus network. This has tremendous potential for in-house generation of graphics, sales charts, diagrams, flowcharts, and books and articles without having to use specialists for final production, bringing the entire process under the control of the documents' creators. The benefits of this approach are less turnaround time, decreased cost, more sensitivity to detail because of greater ownership of the final product, and more creativity, due to increased availability of the tools.

Macintosh Applications

Applications enable the Macintosh to function as any of a variety of tools—pallette, typewriter, ledger, and some that have no previous analog. This part of the book will discuss the major Macintosh applications, and bring a critical eye to how each was designed. We will cover unique features, evaluate the effectiveness of each tool, and provide some real examples of use. This material will enable you to see how using Macintosh applications might look in your everyday life.

12

Word Processing

See What You Get

Word processing programs are applications specially designed for the entry, editing and formatting of text. On machines without a pointing device such as the mouse, editing must be carried out by moving the cursor about the screen with cursor control keys. Usually a block of text must be moved by inserting control characters before and after the block, and then selecting a Copy or Move function by hitting a special key. As we discussed in chapter 4, the mouse greatly simplifies the task of editing text by enabling the user to point directly to an area of the text and **select it,** and then move or copy it to other parts of the document.

Formatting refers to the ability to present the text on the final printed page in a visually organized manner. For instance, text can be **justified,** or evenly aligned, **tabs** can be used to align columns of words or numbers, and portions of the text can be given certain characteristics, such as a bold face or an italic font. Often, these various formats are only completely apparent when the document is printed. Italics, for instance, are not included in the character generators on most terminals, so they will not appear on the screen. On word processors that work in this manner, a control code is inserted in the text, and its presence signifies that a format change has occurred.

Recently, word processors have been moving in the direction of showing the user what the document will look like as it is formatted. Before the advent of bitmapped displays, this could only be an approximation, due to inescapable differences in the characters generated by the video and the printer. The **Xerox Alto** computer (see Appendix A) pioneered the use of a bitmap to display exactly what the user will see at print time with its **BRAVO** editor. BRAVO was the first solid example of what is often called the what-you-see-is-what-you-get style of word processor.

The Mac is the first machine to bring the virtues of bitmapped word processing to a mass audience. Two word processing products have been announced: **MacWrite** by Apple, and Microsoft's entry, **Word for the Macintosh.** First, let's take a detailed look at MacWrite.

MacWrite

MacWrite builds upon the universal editing functions that we discussed in Chapter 9, and adds page formatting features and the ability to search for a specified text string in a document. Under page formatting is included such parameters as tabs, line spacing, margins, indentation and whether text is aligned left, center or right. Text is accumulated as it is entered in memory, and there is no provision for storing part of a file on disk while the rest is in memory. This means that you can enter at most 5,000 words of text in a single file, because that's all that memory allows in a 128K Mac.

This limit will increase significantly when 512K Macs are available, but will still pose a problem for really major word-processing work in that large documents must be broken up into pieces. It also has disadvantages with respect to data security, because if power is lost on the computer while entering text in MacWrite, you will lose any work done since the last time you explicitly saved your work to disk. Another drawback is that page numbers must be manually calculated at each transition between one document and the next. Rumor has it that Apple is working on a second version of MacWrite that will use the disk during editing, and enable much larger documents to be created.

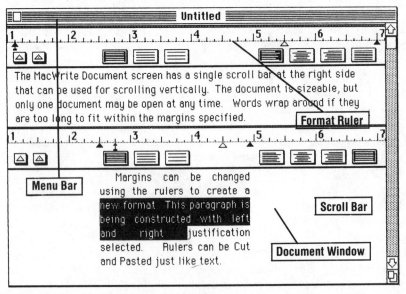

Figure 12.1 The MacWrite Document Window.

With these caveats, however, MacWrite is impressive as a small, cleanly designed and easy-to-understand word processor that exemplifies all of the best features of Macintosh user interface design. Figure 12-1 shows the MacWrite screen when you first start up, with an empty document. The window has a scroll bar only in the vertical direction. The File menu handles the standard set of file operations as discussed in chapter 11. Since MacWrite is a single-document application, you most close the document that you're currently working on before you can open another. A **Page Setup** item (see Figure 12-2) allows you to print on several different sizes of paper, and can even print text sideways on the page (much of this flexibility owes to the bitmap.)

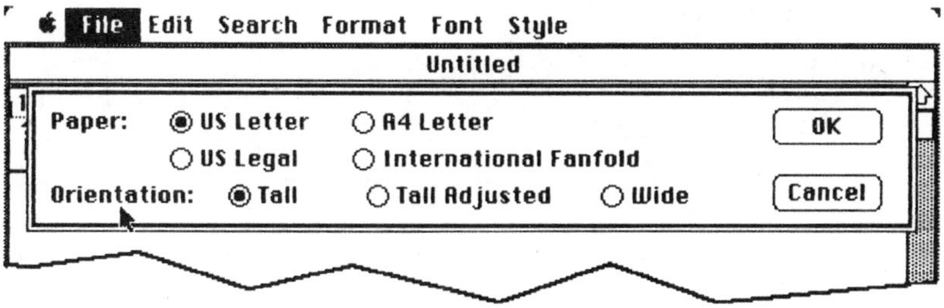

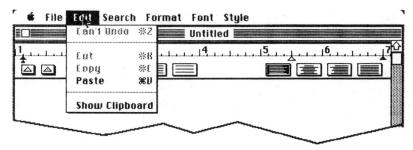

Figure 12.2 The Page Setup Item on the File Menu.

Editing Features

The edit menu (Figure 12-3) supports the old favorites Cut, Copy and Paste, and also supports a single-level Undo function. Undo works as follows: you can always reverse the results of the last action that you took, whether it was typing, a format change, or a command from any menu but the File

Figure 12.3 The MacWrite Edit Menu.

menu. If you deleted some text that you want back, Undo will bring it back for you. Pressing Undo again will then Undo the Undo, and re-delete the text. Hitting Undo multiple times consecutively goes back and forth between keeping and reversing the last action that you took before the Undo. Thus you can't use Undo to retrieve a copy of a document from three versions ago, but you can use it save yourself a lot of grief.

The **Search** menu (Figure 12-4) enables you to search for a text string within the document, and optionally, to replace it with another string. When found, the string will be selected and highlighted, at which point you can replace it either from the change string (by hitting one of the **Change** dialog buttons) or from the Clipboard. Of course, you can always enter text from the keyboard to replace the current selection. The search function has

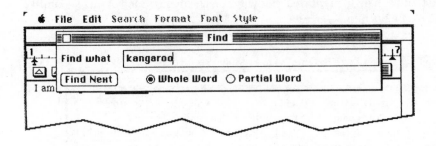

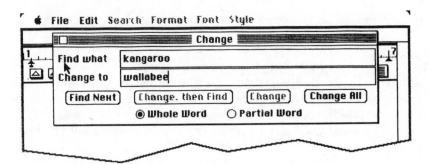

Figure 12.4 The Find and Change Dialogs.

no "wildcard" option, which would allow you to specify patterns of characters to be matched, some of which can be arbitrary characters. This can be a very powerful technique, useful for generating documents from templates automatically. Another desirable feature would be the ability to search for type styles (such as all boldfaced words.)

Formatting With Rulers

Before we go on to the **Format** menu, we need to look at **rulers** (see Figure 12-5). Rulers are an extremely elegant and concise construct that present page format settings in a clear, visual manner. This is where the power of MacWrite lies, because format settings that are obscure on most word processors are a breeze with rulers. You can look at a ruler and immediately translate to its effect on succeeding text; nothing is hidden (unless you explicitly hide the rulers.)

A ruler determines how the text that follows it will be formatted, in terms of its line spacing, alignment, margins and tabs. For instance, to center align all following text, you move the pointer to the box showing centered lines and click—that's all! This will remain in effect until another

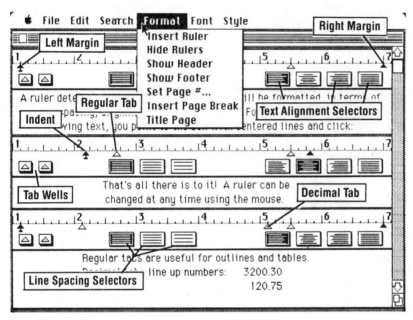

Figure 12.5   A Ruler and its Parts.

ruler is inserted. The same holds true for line spacing. Margins are divided into a left margin marker, an indentation marker that determines the indentation of the first line of a paragraph, and the right margin marker. These are all dragged with the mouse to their desired locations.

Tab stops are dragged from **tab wells** for either regular or decimal tabs. The former left-justify text, while the latter align numbers at their respective decimal points. Once set, tabs can be altered for a given body of text by dragging them to different locations on the ruler or back to the tab well.

Rulers can be inserted anywhere, and moved around via Cut, Copy and Paste. To change the format of a block of text, you need only insert rulers before and after the block, and then set the first ruler up to reflect the new format. Special rulers are available to format header and footer text, with the ability to include date, time and page number. The title page is formatted separately from the rest of the document, and has its own ruler as well.

As is the case with many word processors, in MacWrite you hit the Return key only when you want to start a new paragraph. Line breaks are handled automatically by the program as you type; words are never hyphenated unless you explicitly insert a hyphen followed by a space. Some people may find this lack of hyphenation support to be a problem. I personally prefer no support to being prompted every time that a word could be hyphenated, in the manner of Wordstar™.

Adding Pictures

Pictures can be moved from Macpaint, and embedded in a MacWrite document by Cut, Copy and Paste (Figure 12-6.) You can either Cut or Copy into the Clipboard, for single items, or into the Scrapbook desk accessory, which

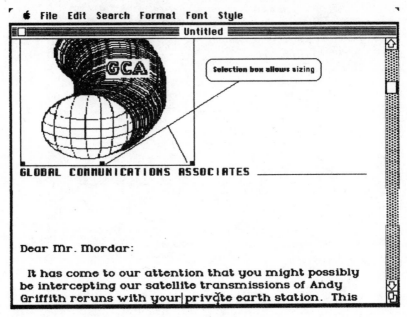

Figure 12.6   A MacPaint Picture in a MacWrite Document.

can hold multiple pictures and text pieces. This ability makes MacWrite really stand out from the crowd, because the heightened impact that embedded pictures can provide is enormous, and very few word processors have the ability to import graphics from other programs (particularly as powerful as Macpaint).

Several fonts are available, and in several different sizes and styles (Figure 12-7.) Because fonts take up a lot of disk space, a utility known as Font Mover is provided by Apple to get rid of the fonts that aren't needed by an application. Very few people will need all of the fonts provided in Mac-Write, and indiscriminate use of many fonts and styles can produce a gaudy, unaesthetic document. The temptation is to overuse these features just because they're available.

The formatting features that become a part of a document created with MacWrite are stripped out when the text is copied to the clipboard and pasted into another application's document. This is quite helpful when telecommunicating text to another computer, because the other computer won't be disturbed by a lot of strange formatting codes that aren't part of its system. Thus, a document could be copied to the clipboard in MacWrite and then pasted in MacTerminal, which could send it to a remote computer

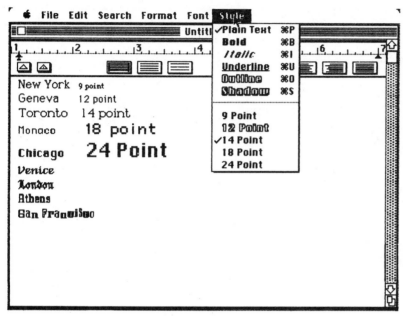

Figure 12.7 Text Fonts and Styles in MacWrite.

running Wordstar. Some time would have to be spent in Wordstar reformatting the document, but at least you'd be starting with clean text. The negative side of this feature is that text also loses its special formats when moved from Macwrite to MacPaint, and vice-versa.

Printing

Printing is supported for the Imagewriter printer in three modes (Figure 12-8.) High quality mode uses the high-resolution mode of the printer, and is significantly slower than the other modes. It produces characters that are actually bolder and fuller than those on the screen, but they're not necessarily clearer. I prefer the Standard mode, which is more or less an exact image of the screen, for a good compromise between clarity and speed.

In summary, MacWrite is an extremely easy to use word processor that should do fine for most work, but is probably inadequate in its present form for very large jobs, or specialized tasks such as form letter generation. It would be greatly improved if it used the disk to handle larger documents, did periodic backup saves automatically, supported multiple document windows, and had more complete Find/Replace and hyphenation support.

Even with these limitations, I prefer it to any word processing application that I've seen, save LisaWrite. The directness and simplicity provided by the mouse and Rulers make editing and formatting a joy, and permit more

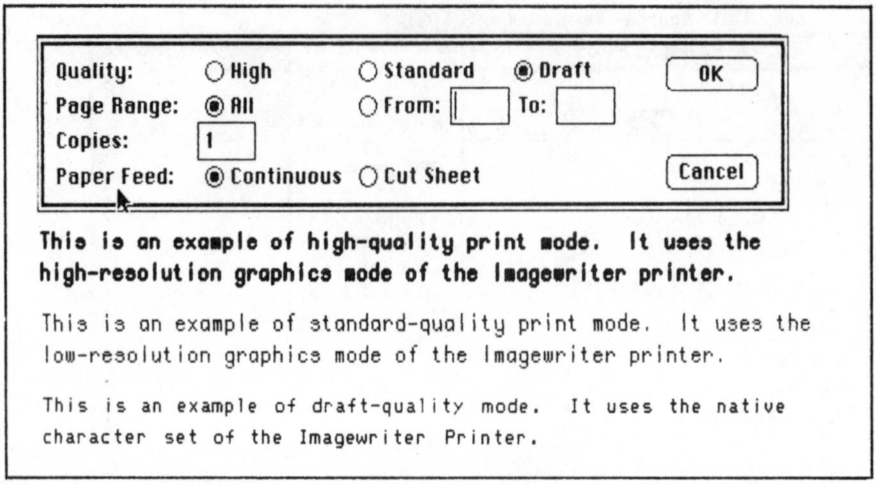

Figure 12.8   The Print Dialog and Examples of Printed Text.

thought to go into the content of the document that might otherwise have been directed into logistics. And if it is a fact that Apple is readying version 2 of MacWrite, it could be a much improved product and a tough one to beat.

Word

Microsoft's Word is a more serious product, both more capable as a word processor than MacWrite and more difficult to learn. Figure 12-9 shows the menu bar and the document window. You'll notice that it has both vertical and horizontal scrolling, as opposed to MacWrite, which has only vertical and is limited to 7½″ of text on a page. Word supports multiple document windows, and uses the disk to hold overflow text that won't fit into memory. Thus, document size would be limited only by disk space, and much larger documents can be edited with Word than MacWrite.

According to a Microsoft spokesman, Word's formatting features also set it apart from MacWrite. Word uses rulers, but they provide more flexibility with tabs, nested paragraphs, margins and indents. A **Glossary** function enables you to keep pieces of "boilerplate" text around as named units, and then include a piece by entering only its name in the document. There is also a built-in mail merge function that can include other documents inside the current one with alterable parameters, a facility that can be used to automate mailing lists, legal documents, and similar repetitive document generation tasks. Microsoft also is committed to support of a "letter-quality" printer, according to their spokesman, by the second release of the product.

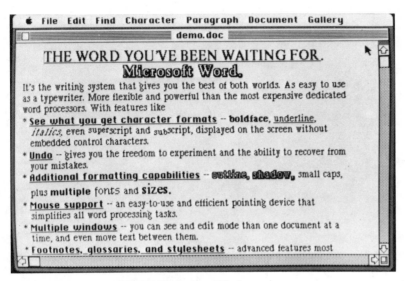

Figure 12.9 The Microsoft Word Document Window.

Word uses a combination of ruler and dialog box to set page formatting parameters. Left and right indent can be set to fractions of an inch for a paragraph, and the spacing before, in and after the paragraph all are set in a dialog. The ruler is used to provide visual cues for margins and indent, and can be used to modify those parameters directly. Ruler scales can be in centimeters, picas, or inches, all available as Options on the Edit menu. Tabs are available for left, right, centered and decimal modes; they are set by pointing to the ruler with the mouse and clicking. Formatting properties can be set separately for characters, paragraphs, and the entire document.

Multiple windows can be used in Word to have different views of the same or different documents. This feature is immensely helpful when editing a book containing references to other chapters or other parts of the same document. Word does not show the document exactly as it will appear when printed, as does MacWrite. Instead, such items as page headers and footers and page breaks are left to print time. A preview mode allows you to see true formats, but you can't make any changes in this mode.

While Word is much more suitable for serious word-processing work than is the first version of MacWrite, it is also more difficult to learn. A couple of hours with MacWrite are probably sufficient to become an expert with it. Word is less transparently designed, partly because some of its features are much more powerful. If you need those features, than you don't have much choice as to which application to use; but be prepared for a few evenings of exploration before you feel really competent with the tool.

13

An Artist's Studio at Your Fingertips

MacPaint

The MacPaint application is a fine demonstration of the power and flexibility of the QuickDraw graphics package as well as the Macintosh user interface. This product transforms the Mac into an "art machine" that is highly tuned and optimized for performing its major functions—producing, editing and saving electronic art. What's most impressive is the parsimony and elegance of the package, which builds upon the mouse techniques learned in the desktop to create a very tight, visually clear, easily assimilated control structure. MacPaint is going to sell a lot of Macs, because it's just so much fun to use and easy to learn quickly (in minutes).

MacPaint vs. LisaDraw

The emphasis in MacPaint is definitely on art and creative work rather than so-called "business graphics", meaning charts, graphs and the like. If you put MacPaint and the graphics package for the Lisa, LisaDraw, alongside each other, this distinction becomes very apparent. Both have the ability to create pictures from primitive shapes—lines, rectangles, polygons and ovals. LisaDraw keeps each new primitive that you add as a separate item, which can then be moved or resized without disturbing what was underneath. In MacPaint, once you add something to the screen, it blends in with what was there before, and cannot be treated as a separate item, much like it would be if you were using a real canvas. This is advantageous (usually) to an artist, who often wants to blend images, but is a drawback if you're building charts or graphs. Also, LisaDraw is line-oriented, whereas MacPaint uses "brushes" that can "paint" patterns on the screen. Apple is developing a version of LisaDraw for the Macintosh that will have more of a business graphics orientation than does MacPaint.

Online Help

Figure 13-1 shows the **Introduction** screen, which is accessible at any time from the **Goodies** menu (Figure 13-2.) The Introduction points out the roles of each of the icons on the left side of the screen. These form the

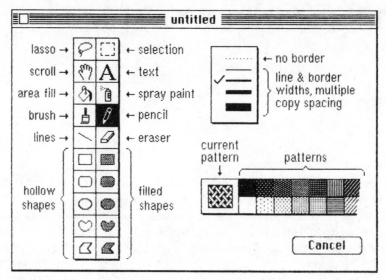

Figure 13.1   The Introduction Screen in MacPaint.

Figure 13.2   The Goodies Menu.

"control panel" for MacPaint, and give immediate access to the bulk of its functions. The one in black is the currently selected function, and can be changed by clicking another icon with the mouse. I was able to use most of these before I had even looked at the manual or the Introduction, just by trying each of them out. With the manual, I would place training time for the whole package at somewhere under two hours, and maybe less than one.

Drawing Tools

The **pencil** draws thin lines, with no "rubber-banding", and the **brush** is used to cover an area with the currently selected **pattern.** All of the pre-defined patterns are lined up on the bottom, and can be selected by clicking with the mouse. You can also define your own pattern in a blown-up box made for that purpose. The shapes on the left marked "filled shapes" automatically fill themselves with the current pattern when you are done sizing them. All of the shapes and lines "rubber-band", meaning that you click once to set the position for one of the vertices, and the shape then follows the pointer around, changing size, until you click again and nail down the other vertex. **Polygons** (bottom of the column) are just a series of rubber-band lines that keep chaining together until you double-click. The

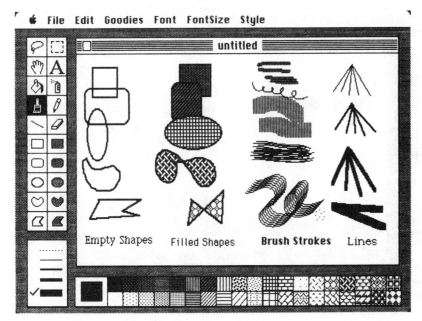

Figure 13.3   Some of the MacPaint Graphics Primitives.

shapes' border lines are drawn in the thickness chosen within the box at the lower left of the screen. Figure 13-3 shows some examples of the various shapes.

A variety of brush shapes is available (see Figure 13-4,) giving a range of realistic effects. The **spray paint** icon gives a very authentic airbrush effect for shading broad areas (Figure 13-5.) The **paint bucket** will fill an enclosed area with the current pattern (and, like the real thing, will paint the entire screen if there are any "leaks").

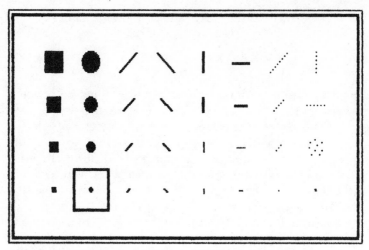

Figure 13.4   Brush Shapes Available in MacPaint.

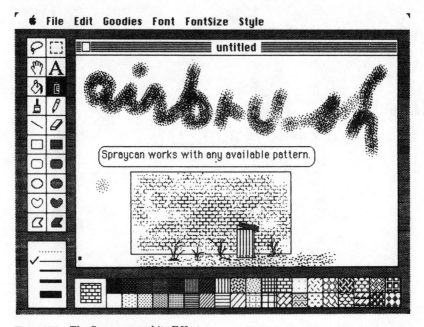

Figure 13.5   The Spraycan and its Effects.

Editing and Copying

The **lasso and selection box** are used to select parts of the drawing for various editing purposes. In the case of the lasso, you draw freehand around an arbitrary region, at which point you can edit, move or copy it. Once selected, a region can be operated upon by the usual editing commands Cut, Copy and Paste. If you drag with the mouse, you can move the region to another point on the screen, and if you hold down the Option key while dragging, you will leave a copy in its original position while dragging another (see Figure 13-6.)

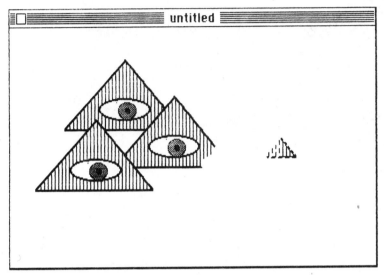

Figure 13.6   Making Copies and Moving Pieces with the Lasso.

Holding down both the Command and Option keys while dragging produces **continous copies** of the region, resulting in an interesting effect (Figure 13-7.) The selection rectangle selects a rectangular region of the

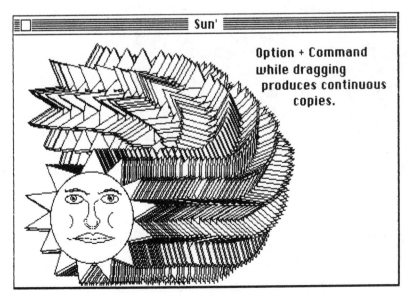

Figure 13.7   An Example of Continuous Copies Mode.

document, and permits all of the manipulations of the lasso in addition to allowing you to resize the region by dragging while holding down the Command key. The image will be sized to the resulting rectangle when the button is released.

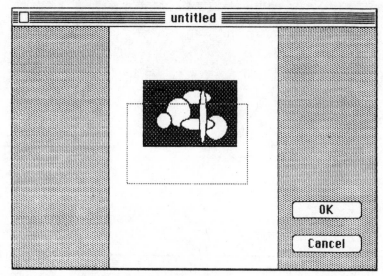

Figure 13.8 Setting the Current View Window.

The **hand icon** can be used to move your drawing around on the page. The Mac screen occupies about a third of a printed page, and you can use the hand to move the portion of the page that the screen shows. Double-

Font	FontSize	Style	
New York	9 point	✓Plain	⌘P
Geneva	✓12	Bold	⌘B
Toronto	14	Italic	⌘I
Monaco	18	Underline	⌘U
✓Chicago	24	Outline	⌘O
	36	Shadow	⌘S
	48		
	72	✓Align Left	⌘L
		Align Middle	⌘M
		Align Right	⌘R

Figure 13.9 Text Font, Size and Style Menus.

clicking the hand icon brings up a screen that enables you to adjust the relative positions of the image, the printed page, and the current viewing window (see Figure 13-8.) A MacPaint image can be a maximum size of 8½″ by 11″.

The letter A indicates a text entry. When you select this icon, a blinking text insertion bar will appear on the screen, and what you type on the keyboard will be inserted at the bar in the currently selected font, size, and style (See Figure 13-9.) Text can be set to automatically align from where the cursor was first placed to the left, center or right. Once placed, text cannot be moved as a separate entity; it becomes a part of the painting, like anything else that is drawn. You can always move it with the lasso or selection box, but you must exercise great care if it is over an existing pattern or figure.

Other Features

Any section of the drawing can be selected and then blown up in **FatBits mode,** which makes the individual dots very large for precise manipulation (Figure 13-10.) In this mode, the pencil, eraser and brush can be used to

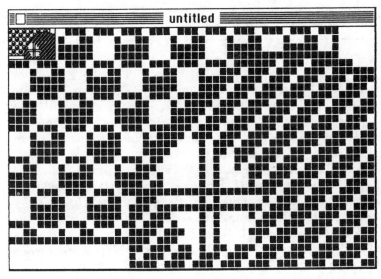

Figure 13.10 Using Fatbits for Fine Work.

alter the individual dots to either black or white. While in FatBits, the window can be scrolled around using the hand to any portion of the originally selected region. This mode can also be use for very precise positioning of the lasso or selection box over a delicate piece of the drawing, because it easily gives single-dot resolution. Because of the rather clumsy nature of the mouse for freehand drawing, you will very often find yourself taking a rough stab at a section of the image with the mouse in normal mode, and then touching up individual dots with FatBits. It's a good solution to what could be a very annoying problem.

An eraser is available to clear unwanted pieces of the drawing, and the entire screen can be cleared by double-clicking the eraser icon. Undo is

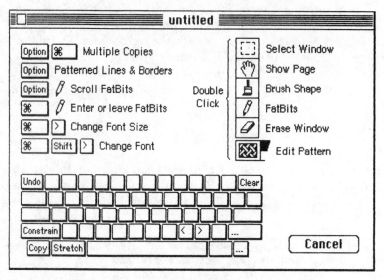

Figure 13.11   The Shortcuts Screen in MacPaint.

available from the Edit menu to retract an unwanted operation, like clearing the screen. A section can be selected and inverted, which turns all black dots to white and vice versa, as well as rotated in 90 degree increments and flipped horizontally or vertically. You can also trace the edges of any figure, creating another outline of it around its periphery.

Brush movement is normally freehand, but can be constrained by holding down the shift key to move either horizontally or vertically, which is handy near the outlines of rectangles. Brush motions can be mirrored in any of four axes, which places symmetrical duplicates of anything you draw in other areas of the screen. This can produce some really spectacular effects when all four axes are enabled, because symmetry appears where none was intended. Figure 13-13 shows an example of some electronic scribbling using brush mirrors.

Shortcuts

Although the mouse alone can accomplish 90 percent of what is commonly needed, the keyboard is used to enter text, provide a shortcut method of simulating some mouse actions, and provide a few specialized functions. The shortcuts page (see Figure 13-11) shows which keys are used for these

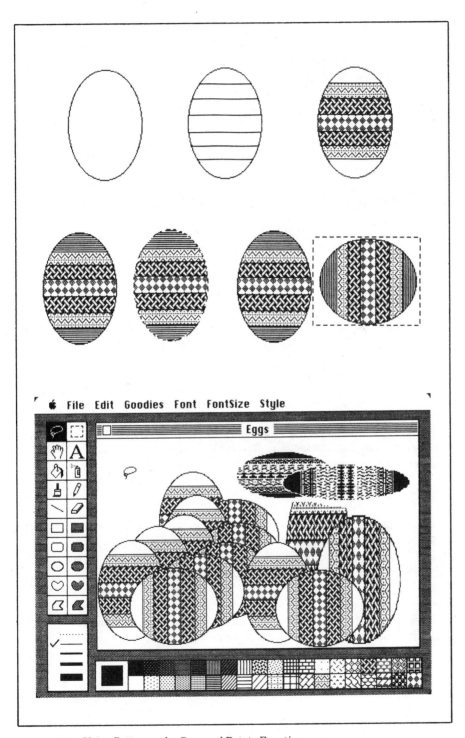

Figure 13.12 Using Patterns, the Copy and Rotate Functions.

various purposes. Holding down Options while dragging a selected area of the drawing produces an exact copy of the selected piece, which you can then drag to another part of the illustration. When the button is released, the copy blends into the background, and cannot be separated from it again. The shift key, if depressed while moving the brush or pencil, or dragging an image, will constrain movement to a vertical or horizontal direction. This is very for eliminating the shakiness that is a natural accompaniment to drawing with the mouse. Figures 13-12 to 13-14 show some examples of what can be done with MacPaint by a rank amateur.

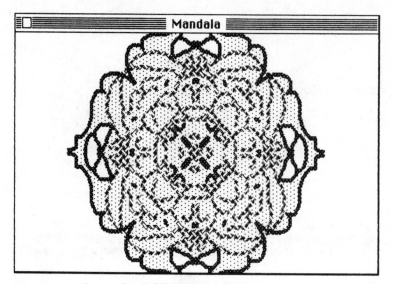

Figure 13.13   A Picture Created Using Brush Mirrors.

Summary

If I had to pick only one application to use with the Macintosh, this would be it. MacPaint is an ideal blend of simplicity and power, and a perfect match for the machine. It clearly doesn't have everything that you might want in a business drawing program, but that wasn't its intent. As a personal tool, MacPaint is just sheer fun. It gives you ideas that wouldn't have occurred if you couldn't experiment and pull out the stops. Being able to Undo the last operation means that you can try just about anything without ruining your drawing, and facilities like multiple copies and mirrored brushes are simply not available in other media. If you want to spend just twenty minutes with a Macintosh, or have one and don't know what to do with it, sit down with MacPaint. You'll be hooked before you know it.

Figure 13.14   A Picture Created Using Various Brush Shapes.

14

Communications

MacTerminal is a product from Apple that provides interactive support for the Mac's serial communications (see Chapter 11.) This application allows the Macintosh to emulate a **terminal,**which is a device containing a keyboard and either a CRT screen or printing capability that is used to access remote computers via communications links. Terminals generally are not programmable devices, and are built to perform the singular task of communicating with a computer.

A Typical Dialup System

(Figure 14-1) shows the components of a typical dialup communications network. There is a relatively powerful computer at a remote location that can service up to several hundred users at one time. It may have several **communications controllers** attached to it that handle the overhead necessary to keep the communications links active. These controllers only bother the main computer when it is needed to either send or receive data. The controller communicates with the outside world by means of modems, which translate the outgoing binary numbers into audible tones that are suitable for sending over ordinary telephone lines, and do the reverse process for incoming data.

Modems

Modems are rated according to their speed, or **baud rate.**The least expensive modems operate at 300 baud, which means that they are capable of sending and receiving about 30 characters per second. These are the most common devices, but recently 1200 baud modems have descended in price to the sub-$500 range, and have gotten much more popular. These modems can handle around 120 characters per second, a fourfold increase over the cheaper devices. Apple has both a 300 and 300/1200 baud modem available for the Macintosh.

In order for the modem to use the telephone line, it must first establish a connection with the host by dialing, just as you would to place an ordinary call. The fanciest modems can do this automatically, and are capable of

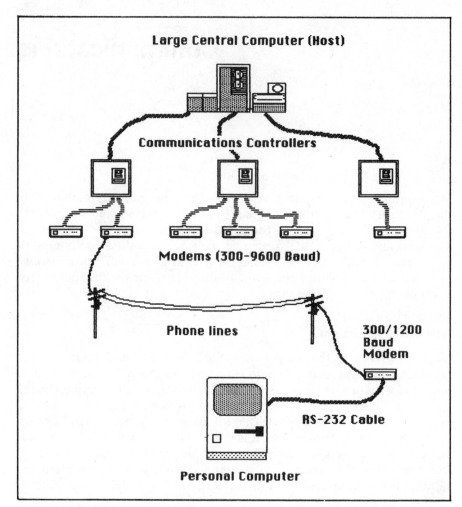

Figure 14.1 The Components in a Typical Communications System.

receiving commands from a computer or terminal telling them what numbers to dial. **Hayes** was one of the first companies to produce a modem with these features, and consequently the set of commands that drive Hayes modems has become something of a standard. The Apple modems are mostly Hayes-compatible, although there are some differences in the more esoteric commands.

The user must have a modem that generates tones compatible with the one used by the host computer. Again, an informal standard has arisen which the Apple and Hayes modems obey (Bell 212-A), making them compatible with almost any host modem. The modem is connected via an RS-232 serial interface (see Chapter 11) to the user's computer or terminal. In general, the serial interface must carry data at the same rate as the modem, either at 300 or 1200 baud. If a terminal is being used, whatever the user types at the keyboard is automatically sent over the serial interface to the modem, and data that the serial line receives is sent to the screen.

Communications Software

If the user has a computer, however, the situation is a little more complicated. Computers have many different I/O devices, and there is no preset connection between any of them as there is between the serial line and the screen of a terminal. **Software** must establish a connection between the devices, which is why communications programs exist. An application such as MacTerminal must be used that reads data from the serial line, sends it to the screen, and reads characters typed at the keyboard, sending them to the modem. Additionally, some of these programs allow you to keep the information that travels over the serial line in a disk file, as well as transmit a file to the host computer.

MacTerminal

(Figure 14-2) shows the MacTerminal window with the File menu pulled down (note: I used a preliminary version of MacTerminal for this material, and some of the features in the final program could look a little different.) The **Get** and **Save Settings** items enable you to configure the baud rate and other parameters for a particular kind of use, and then save them and retrieve them using files. We'll discuss the parameters that can change in a moment. **Save Text** and **Settings** holds the text that has appeared on the screen for the current session in a disk file along with the settings that were used.

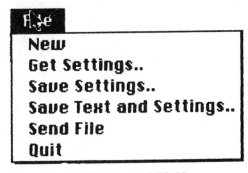

Figure 14.2 The MacTerminal File Menu.

Terminal/Computer Differences

When characters come over the serial line to a terminal, they appear on the screen, and eventually scroll off the top of the screen. At that point, they are lost, and can never be retrieved. One of the advantages of using a computer for communications is that you can capture the characters to a disk file, and later look at them or print them using a word processor. The Macintosh adds a new dimension to this process, because lines that scroll off the top of the window can be retained until memory fills up, and the **scroll bar** at the right of the screen can be used to scroll backward or forward, examining text text that you might need to see again while still logged on to the host.

Whether or not lines scrolled off the top are remembered is a setting that can be changed on the Convenience Settings dialog (Figure 14-3.) Other

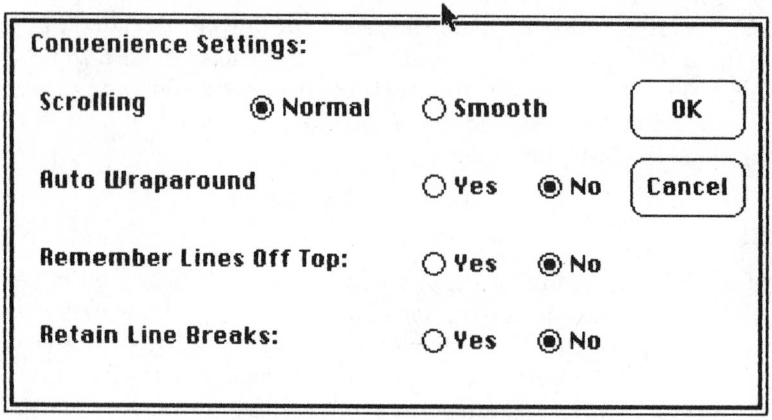

Figure 14.3 Convenience Settings in MacTerminal.

sections of this dialog include: normal/smooth scrolling, which will move lines up either the normal line at a time or a dot at a time, giving the impression of continuous, flowing movement; Auto Wraparound, which drops the cursor to the next line as soon as the right margin is reached; and retain line breaks, which keeps carriage returns as part of the text.

Additionally, the standard **Cut, Copy** and **Paste** commands can be used to move text from the MacTerminal to desk accessories or other documents and pull text in from the clipboard. Thus, you could paste a **standard logon sequence,** (which would normally have to be typed each time) into the Scrapbook, and then Copy it from the Scrapbook into MacTerminal whenever you needed to log on to a particular host computer.

Communications Parameters

Let's look at the terminal settings that must be determined before we can log on to the host. A dialog box enables the settings to be examined or

changed at any time (see Figure 14-4.) The Terminal section permits Mac-
Terminal to emulate one of three types of terminals. The **VT100** and **VT52**
types emulate terminals manufactured by Digital Equipment Corporation
that have received wide use in minicomputer and mainframe applications.
These terminals provide certain specialized functions, like the ability to
move the cursor to a specified location on the screen via a command sequence from the host. The Macintosh can look like one of these devices to
the computer on the other end, enabling it use software that exploits
the unique features of those terminals. The **TTY** type is a catchall for
any other terminal, and doesn't provide any special features like
cursor addressing.

Terminal Setup

Terminal	◉ UT100	○ UT52	○ TTY	
Baud Rate	○ 50	○ 75	○ 110	○ 134.5
	○ 150	○ 200	○ 300	○ 600
	◉ 1200	○ 1800	○ 2000	○ 2400
	○ 3600	○ 4800	○ 9600	○ 19200
Parity	○ Even	○ Odd	◉ None	
Handshake	○ Hon/Hoff	○ Clear To Send	◉ None	
Commmunications	◉ On Line	○ Local		
Character Width	○ 7 Bit:	◉ 8 Bit:	[OK]	[Cancel]

Figure 14.4 The Terminal Settings.

Baud rate provides all of the standard speeds used in RS-232 communications, although only 300 and 1200 baud are likely to be used with modems. MacTerminal works equally well if the Mac is connected to another
computer via only a serial line, without using modems; in this case, the
highest baud rate supported in common by the devices at both ends would
probably be used.

Parity denotes a means of checking each character to see whether it was
altered by a transmission error. There are several methods of parity generation, all of which utilize the last bit in each 8-bit character. Parity checking is far from foolproof, and slows down the software at both ends; consequently, it is often not used. The **Handshake** section determines how
and if a synchronization will be established between the two ends of the
communications line. This is necessary if one end has to do something that
will take a long time, such as a disk write, at which point it must tell the

device on the other end to stop sending until it catches up. Handshaking can be established via either hardware or software, or both.

XON/XOFF is a **software handshaking** protocol that enables the receiving side to tell the transmitting side to stop (XOFF), and later resume (XON.) Each is accomplished by sending a single character. Clear To Send indicates a **hardware handshake** that requires both sides to utilize lines in the serial cable as switches and flags telling each other when transmission is appropriate. This can only be done if there are no modems intervening, because the serial lines terminate at the modem and have no effect on the remote computer. No Handshaking can be used if occasional lost characters are not a problem, particularly if disk capture isn't required.

On Line and Local denote whether characters are sent to the host computer as they are typed (On Line,) or whether they are simply routed to the Macintosh screen. The **Character Width** setting determines whether 7 or 8 bits are sent to the host for each character typed; since Ascii codes only require 7 bits per character, the eighth is superfluous if parity isn't used and can be ignored.

The settings may sound confusing, but it isn't Apple's fault, because they reflect the diversity of methods that the world uses for serial communications. This is one of the least standardized areas in computer technology, and much of it dates back decades to when very different equipment was used. The important thing is that to be able to communicate today, you have to be able to change any of these settings to match those of the host, which are rarely under your control. Fortunately, MacTerminal makes it relatively painless to change the Terminal Settings on the fly, so experimentation is possible.

Possible Uses

Communications provides access to a wide variety of services and contacts that make it well worth the trouble of learning what's what. For example, MCI mail enables its users to compose a letter on a personal computer's word processor, and then dial up a remote computer and send the text of the letter using 300 or 1200 baud communications. The letter will be delivered, printed and in an envelope, in as little as 4 hours. Dialup services such as Compuserve have their own electronic mail facilities as well as hundreds of other subject areas.

This book was prepared on a Lisa 2 using LisaWrite, and then downloaded to an IBM PC using LisaTerminal, which is a very close cousin to MacTerminal. With the help of Tom Casper, President of TelePhotronic Typography in Chicago, we set up a number of 2-to-4 character codes with which he could drive his VIP typesetting machines. Those codes were inserted into our documents using IBM Wordstar, and the documents were telecommunicated to TelePhotronic for typesetting. Often a job was back the same day, because the lengthy and error-prone re-keying process was avoided. We used the PC for the coding step because we had a program that enabled us to redefine some of the PC's keys to produce a character string, which speeded up the entry process because a code became a single keystroke. Hopefully, a facility such as this will be available on the Mac some day.

Using Compuserve

To use a service such as Compuserve, the first step is to set the telephone number that MacTerminal will send to the modem, and which it in turn will dial to establish communications with the host (see Figure 14-5.) Then

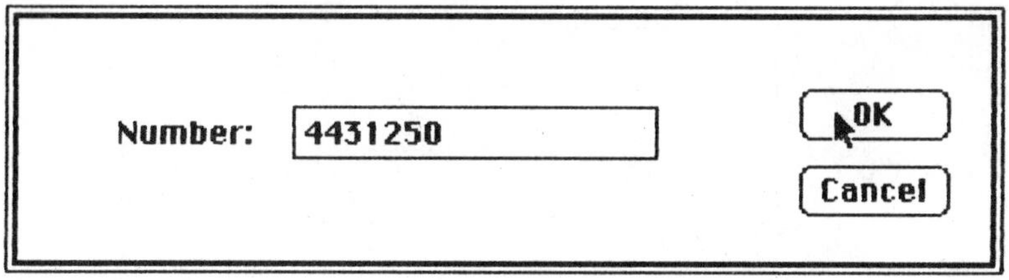

```
    Number:  | 4431250        |        ( ▶OK   )
                                        ( Cancel )
```

Figure 14.5 Setting the Phone Number for a Call.

we choose **Dial** on the Phone menu, at which point the modem dials up the host computer. When carriers have been established, indicated by 2 tones in the speaker of the modem, we can enter the logon sequence for Compuserve, which is Command/C followed by you user ID and password. If both are correct, you're logged on, and presented with the Compuserve main menu. Figure 14-6 shows the Compuserve Home Services menu, listing by category the many useful general-interest services available.

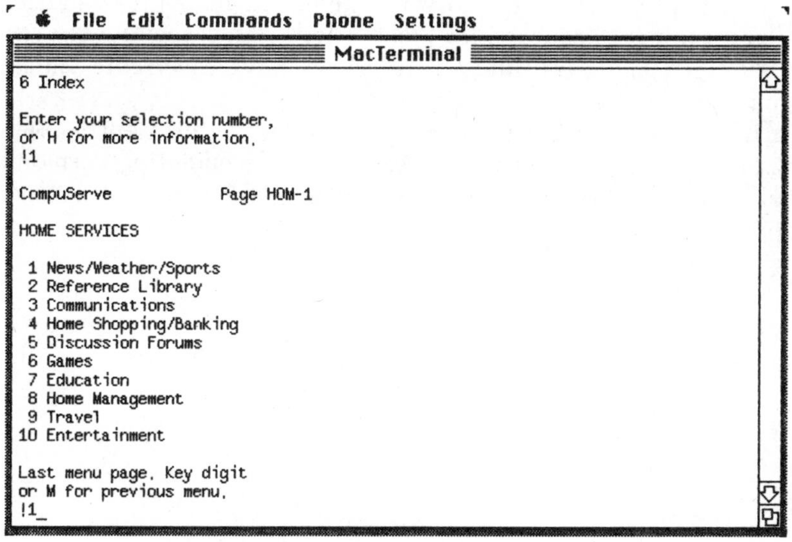

```
 🍎 File  Edit  Commands  Phone  Settings
════════════════ MacTerminal ════════════════
6 Index

Enter your selection number,
or H for more information.
!1

CompuServe            Page HOM-1

HOME SERVICES

 1 News/Weather/Sports
 2 Reference Library
 3 Communications
 4 Home Shopping/Banking
 5 Discussion Forums
 6 Games
 7 Education
 8 Home Management
 9 Travel
10 Entertainment

Last menu page. Key digit
or M for previous menu.
!1_
```

Figure 14.6 The Compuserve Home Services Menu.

A huge body of information is available through such systems as Compuserve and The Source, ranging from making your travel plans to the news to stock quotes. Figure 14-7 shows a sample session in **Compuserve's**

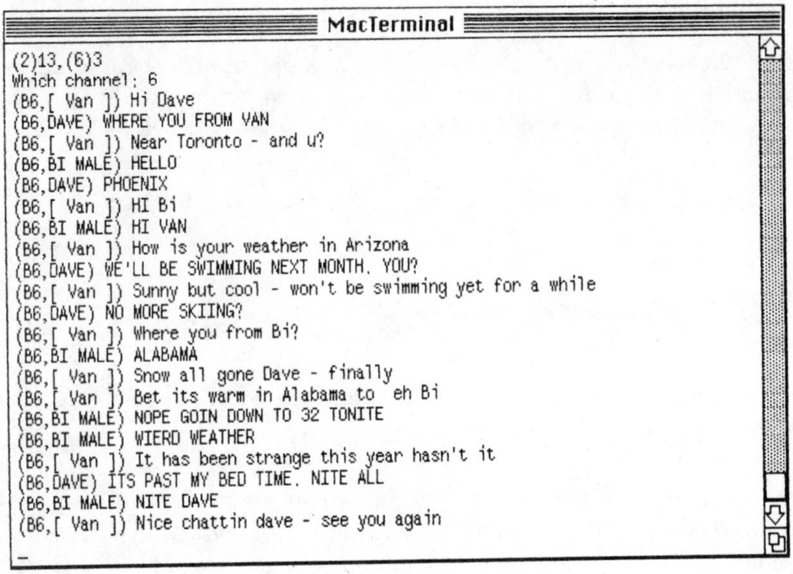

```
≡≡≡≡≡≡≡≡≡≡≡≡≡≡ MacTerminal ≡≡≡≡≡≡
(2)13,(6)3
Which channel: 6
(B6,[ Van ]) Hi Dave
(B6,DAVE) WHERE YOU FROM VAN
(B6,[ Van ]) Near Toronto - and u?
(B6,BI MALE) HELLO
(B6,DAVE) PHOENIX
(B6,[ Van ]) HI Bi
(B6,BI MALE) HI VAN
(B6,[ Van ]) How is your weather in Arizona
(B6,DAVE) WE'LL BE SWIMMING NEXT MONTH. YOU?
(B6,[ Van ]) Sunny but cool - won't be swimming yet for a while
(B6,DAVE) NO MORE SKIING?
(B6,[ Van ]) Where you from Bi?
(B6,BI MALE) ALABAMA
(B6,[ Van ]) Snow all gone Dave - finally
(B6,[ Van ]) Bet its warm in Alabama to  eh Bi
(B6,BI MALE) NOPE GOIN DOWN TO 32 TONITE
(B6,BI MALE) WIERD WEATHER
(B6,[ Van ]) It has been strange this year hasn't it
(B6,DAVE) ITS PAST MY BED TIME. NITE ALL
(B6,BI MALE) NITE DAVE
(B6,[ Van ]) Nice chattin dave - see you again
—
```

Figure 14.7   A Screen from a Compuserve CB Simulation Session.

CB simulation, which allows users to log on, using "handles" as they would in a genuine CB session, and then carry out a multiple-way conversation. It can be quite intriguing to interact with CB'ers from all over the country, knowing them only by their words and often glamorous handles. CB regulars frequently convene for "real" parties after they meet over the computerized airwaves, and CB meetings have reportedly led to several marriages!

For further information: Compuserve, 5000 Arlington Centre, Box 20212, Columbus, OH 43220. The Source: Source Telecomputing Corporation, 1616 Anderson Road, McLean, VA 22102. TelePhotronic, 212 West Superior Street, Chicago, IL. 60610, (312) 944-6944.

15

Business and Finance

In the area of business productivity tools, Microsoft lead the way with **Multiplan** for the Macintosh, which was available when the Mac was announced. Microsoft also announced **Chart,** a business graphics application, and **File,** a database application, but these hadn't been released when we went to print. Other vendors have made announcements that they intend to convert or develop products in this core area for the Mac.

Multiplan

When **VisiCalc™** first took the world by storm, it became the archetypical answer to the question, "What can I do with a personal computer?" More than any other application, the spreadsheet was responsible for bringing thousands of PCs, especially Apple IIs, into mainstream business environments. Many Apple IIs were bought just to run a spreadsheet. VisiCalc provided a novel new way of doing formerly tedious manual tasks, and it could be learned by anyone. It created its own model for user interface design, one so radically different and effective that soon many vendors were forced to accept this model as a de facto standard.

When Microsoft entered the spreadsheet wars with its **Multiplan™,** that product received a lot of favorable reviews for its approach. The first implementations of Multiplan were on non-graphics machines like the Osborne, and couldn't depart too radically from what other vendors had done. But Microsoft was involved in the Macintosh design effort very early on, and had a chance to spend at least a year developing a version of Multiplan that was optimized for the Mac. Microsoft got a long jump on other third-party developers, and they were the only vendor to release a product at Mac announcement time.

Online Help

Multiplan has a well-developed online help system that is available as the first item on the Apple menu (Figure 15-1.) The help text is divided into

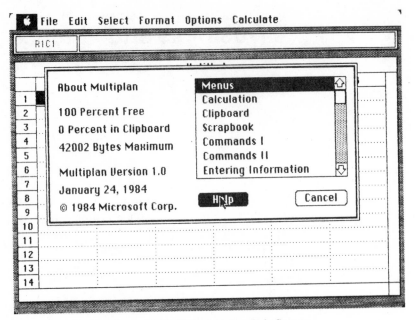

Figure 15.1   The First Screen in Multiplan's Online Help System..

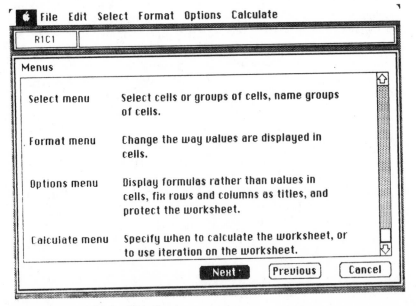

Figure 15.2   A Multiplan Help Screen.

broad topics which can be continuously scrolled within each topic (see Figure 15-2.) This is quite adequate to get started with, and the manual can be used for reference later, when more detail is required. It's very easy to interrupt your work and get into the help system, and the material seems to be fairly well organized.

One could easily write a book on Multiplan alone, because it's a very complete program with lots of bells and whistles. Here, I'll concentrate on the special touches that make it stand out against the competition, and any drawbacks that I've noticed. Figure 15-3 shows the Multiplan document

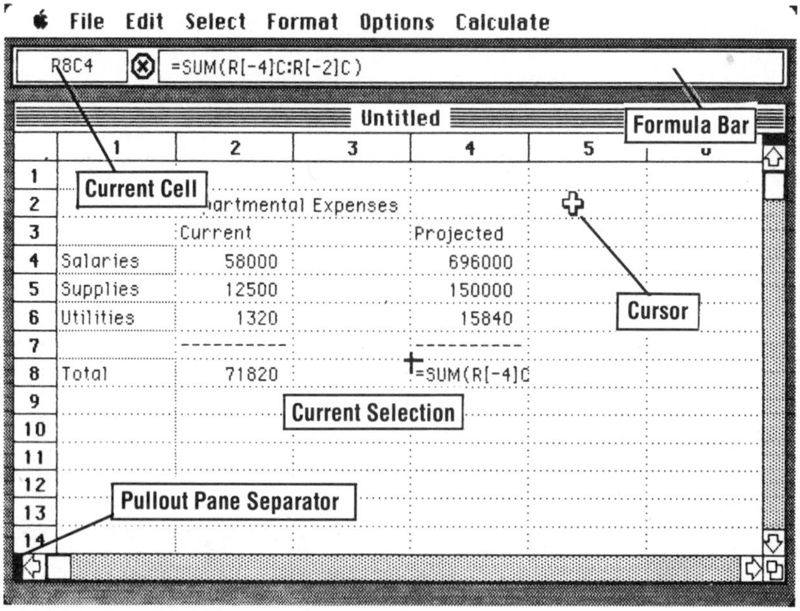

Figure 15.3 The Multiplan Document Window.

window and points out the high points of its geography. The **formula bar** has the current cell indicator on the left, and a box that holds the formula for the current cell on the right. By the way, in case you aren't familiar with **spreadsheets,** the basic idea is that the document is divided into cells, each of which can hold a number, string or formula. Formulas can include other cells in them, such as **R4C2 +** R4C3, which means "the contents in row 4 column 2 plus the contents of row 4 column 3".

Formula Bar

Here's how the formula bar works: You move the mouse around and click it in the spreadsheet to select the cell(s) that you want, at which point you can start typing to enter a formula, number or text. Once you type a character, you're in **Edit mode,** indicated by the **Cancel Icon** becoming visible. This changes the effect of clicking the mouse: you can now use the mouse to enter the values of cells in your formula by simply moving the pointer to the desired cell and clicking. While this is extremely convenient, the switching between select mode and edit mode takes some getting used to. I found myself frequently selecting cells while still in edit mode, causing spurious cell names to get inserted into the current cell's formula.

Cell References

Entering cell addresses by pointing with the mouse causes the references to be entered as **relative** rather than **absolute.**This means that instead of the cell's address (R4C2) Multiplan uses the cell's distance from the current selection. For instance, R [-4] C [2] refers to the cell that is 4 rows up and 2 columns to the right from the current selection. Relative references are useful when formulas are copied, because then the cell often doesn't have to change, as long as everything is in the same relative position. References can always be converted back to absolute using the Edit menu.

Of course there's always Undo on the Edit menu, which comes in very handy at times like that. Ultimately, being able to enter cell addresses by clicking makes it worth the extra care that must be taken with the modes. While in Edit mode, you have the standard editing functions available, and the insertion bar behaves as usual. To exit to command/selection mode, you can either hit Return, which causes the formula bar to be plugged into the current cell, or you can hit the Cancel Icon, which cancels the latest edits that were performed.

The mouse is a natural for spreadsheets. It's simply wonderful to be able to move the pointer around and select cells. Clicking selects a single cell, and dragging can be used to select a rectangle. To copy a group of cells, you select them with the mouse, select Copy on the Edit menu, then move to the target location, select it and choose Paste from the Edit menu. To select an entire column or row, just point to the number in the margin and select it.

User Interface Features

While the mouse handling in Multiplan coincides with Apple's User Interface Guidelines, some extra twists have been added by Microsoft that add a degree of convenience. For instance, when you click in the grey area of the scroll bar, the elevator box starts moving toward the pointer at page intervals, pausing momentarily at each page. This methodology is more convenient than other methods of page scrolling that I've seen, because it requires the least mouse movement. Also, the pointer takes on several different symbols as you move it in the various regions of the window, and each shape is well chosen to convey the function of the mouse at that point.

Column width can be visually adjusted by moving the pointer to the upper margin line and dragging the right edge of the column to the new width. Column widths can also be set in the Format menu for a selected group of columns (Figure 15-4.) The document window can be scrolled both horizontally and vertically, and Figure 15-5 shows how the screen may be divided into up to four **panes** displaying separate areas of the spreadsheet.

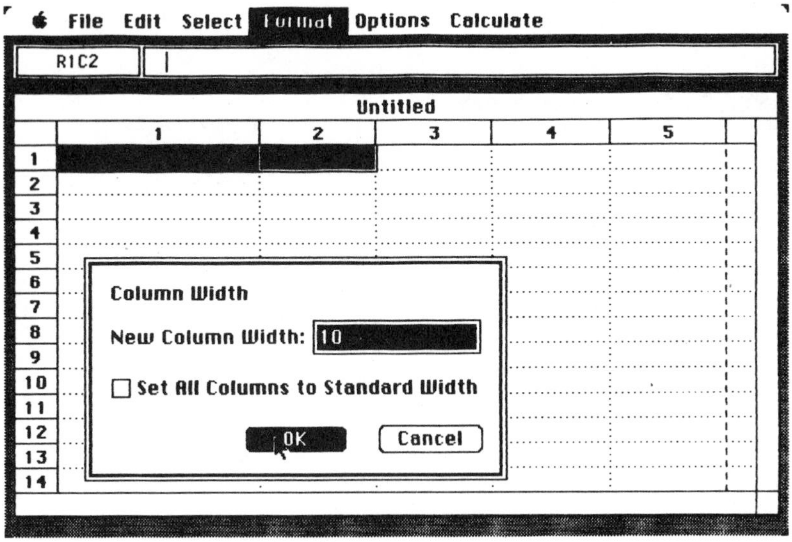

Figure 15.4   Setting the Column Width for a Selection.

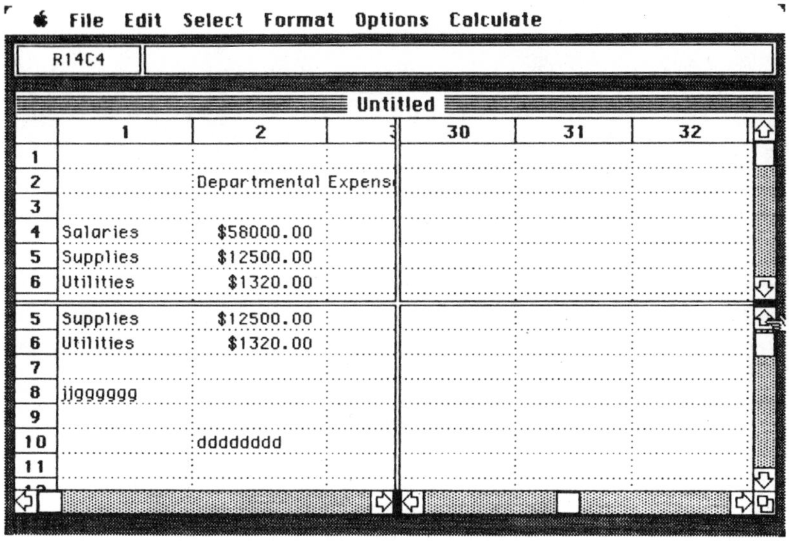

Figure 15.5   A Spreadsheet Divided Into Panes.

Horizontal scrolling is completely independent between panes, but vertical scrolling is locked for the left and write quadrants opposite each other. The left half can't be on a separate set of rows from the right half.

Formatting

Inserting a row or column is as simple as holding down the shift key and clicking, for a single insertion, or dragging to insert a range. The Cut item can be used to delete a range of cells. (Figure 15-6) shows the items avail-

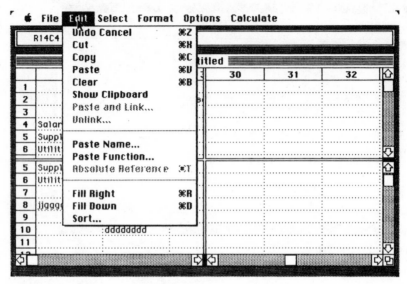

Figure 15.6 The Edit Menu.

able on the Edit menu. In addition to the standard editing commands, there are some powerful features here that are worthy of mention. **Paste and link** allows you to paste into a spreadsheet, while at the same time Linking

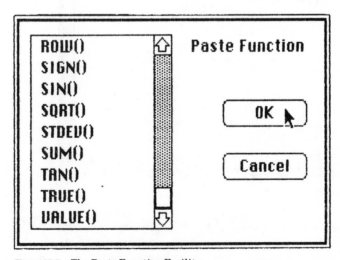

Figure 15.7 The Paste Function Facility.

to the spreadsheet from which the Clipboard contents came. Linking causes a cell reference to be made to a separate spreadsheet file, enabling much larger spreadsheet networks to be developed than memory would ordinarily permit. **Paste Name** allows a name to be selected from a list that assigns user-defined symbolic names to a range of cells. Thus, you could assign the range R2C5:R8C10 the name Fred, and then use Fred from then on as a symbolic shorthand for that range of cells.

Sort enables you to sort a series of rows in ascending or descending order. This can be useful for alphabetizing titles, or generating ordered lists of amounts. Because sorting rearranges cells, it can throw off formulas that reference those cells, a warning that is made very clear in the Multiplan manual.

Paste Function allows you to select one of many built-in functions for use in a formula (see Figure 15-7.) The list is reasonably complete, and is comparable to the other top spreadsheet products. A unique feature is **ITERCNT(),** which, together with the conditional IF() functions provides a looping facility, and makes it possible to create programmable structures of cells. Also distinctive are a set of **string functions** that allow specialized manipulation of text.

The Format menu (Figure 15-8) allows cells to be represented in a variety of formats, including some useful for scientific and engineering

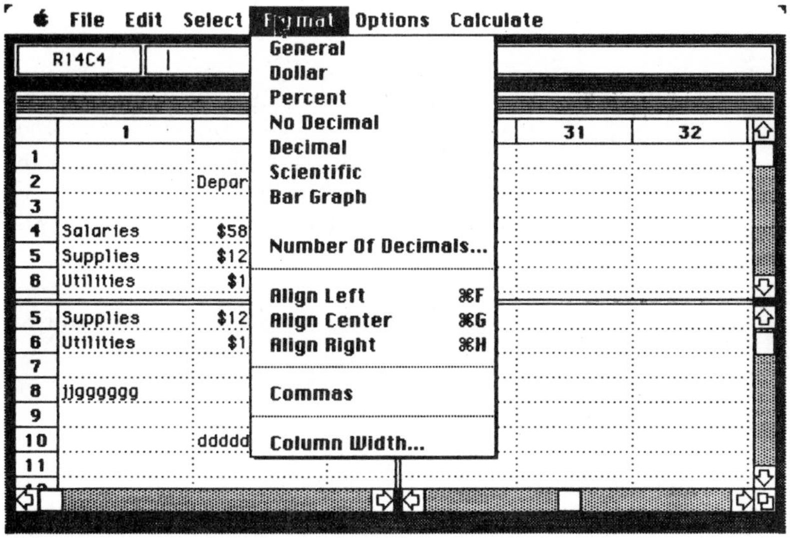

Figure 15.8   The Format Menu.

applications. The **Options menu** (Figure 15-9) enables you to freeze a range of rows and columns as titles, fixing them so that they won't scroll with the rest of the spreadsheet. Set and Remove Page Break enable you to explicitly control when the printer ejects a page during the printing of your worksheet. Other options allow protection of the entire document as well as individual cells from inadvertent or unwanted modification. A **password** can be associated with a spreadsheet that prevents unauthorized access.

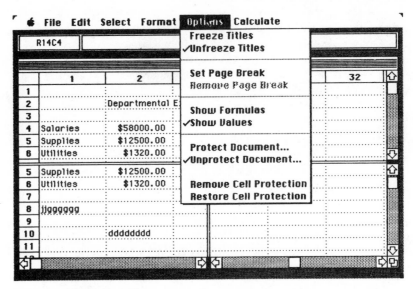

Figure 15.9   The Options Menu.

Documentation

Finally, a word about the low-tech part of Multiplan—the manual. The Multiplan paper documentation is clear, concise, and logically organized, and liberally decorated with screens printed directly from the Macintosh. It seems that the effort of developing on the Macintosh forces a certain clarity of design which can have a positive influence on the written documentation. Even so, the Multiplan manual is to be commended as an exceptional job. While it isn't as flashy as Apple's very high-quality manuals, it is at least as informative nd generally somewhat less condescending in tone.

Summary

Multiplan is a well-designed and executed package that uses the power of the Macintosh user interface to great advantage. The mouse brings a whole new dimension of ease to working with spreadsheets, as it does with other areas of human-computer endeavor. Microsoft has directed a considerable amount of attention into details on this product, no doubt intending it to be their showpiece for the near future. At the moment, Multiplan is the only game in town, and it will create a very high standard for the competition. I found it much preferable to any of the conventional, non-mouse technology spreadsheets that I've used on other machines. But don't take my word for it—try it out!

Other Business Products

Microsoft has announced two other business tools for the Macintosh, **Chart** and **File.** Chart is a tool that enables the user to develop business graphics and assemble them into pages suitable for presentation (see Figure 15-10.) File is a database manager that utilizes windows to provide different views of the data (see Figure 15-11.)

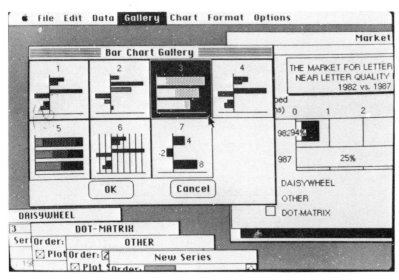

Figure 15.10   Microsoft Chart for the Macintosh.

Software Publishing Corp. has announced plans to develop its popular **PFS:FILE** and **PFS:REPORT** tools for the Macintosh. PFS:FILE is a database application that has filing, sorting and searching capabilities. Its emphasis is upon enabling the user to design data entry forms on the screen that resemble paper forms such as invoices or personnel records. A search capability enables the user to find a subset of the database by entering logical combinations of search criteria. PFS:REPORT expands upon the reporting capabilities of PFS:FILE, by summarizing the information and performing user-pecified calculations upon it. Both programs will utilize the Macintosh mouse/window user interface. Each package will have a suggested retail price of around $100.

Lotus Corp. has announced a major product for the Mac that will probably be an integrated package along the lines of 1-2-3. Other major developers reported to be working on products include Continental Software, Hayden Software, Kriya Systems, DB Master Associates and many others. Although developing an application for the Mac has proven to be a significant resource investment, there is a solid base of commitment among major software developers to tailor successful products for this machine. The Mac is never any easy conversion, which is beneficial in that it enforces a rethinking of design issues, particularly in the area of the user interface.

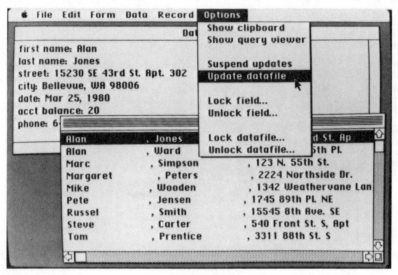

Figure 15.11 Microsoft File for the Macintosh.

The Toolbox:
Building
Your Own

This section will go behind the scenes for a look at some of the
Macintosh systems software from which applications are built.
First we will introduce the Toolbox, a tremendous body
of support code that exists in the Macintosh ROM.
Then we will examine how building programs on the Mac
will look using a variety of languages.

16

The User Interface Toolbox

Nuts and Bolts

This section is going to be a little more technical, so bear with me if you aren't very technically oriented. One of the joys of using the Mac is that you really don't need to know much about its inner workings to have an extremely profitable experience with it. But if you're a person who is interested in building your own applications, there's a lot that you need to know, because the Macintosh systems software is voluminous; this section will give you an overview of what's there, so that you can take more enlightened steps toward creating your own programs if you so desire. If you don't know much about how computers work, but are very curious, you can follow along, perhaps looking up words that you don't understand in the Glossary.

When one steps back and takes a look at the depth and detail of the Macintosh user interface, with its menus, windows, icons, dialogs, and other features, the task of writing an application that can function in this environment seems overwhelming.

OS and Toolbox

Apple has built the Macintosh systems software in two levels: The **Operating System** (OS), which handles the hardware devices, memory, and the file system; and the **User Interface Toolbox,** which adds an extremely powerful library of user-callable routines to handle windows, menus, drawing in the bitmap, and the like. What the Toolbox provides is a "**Virtual Machine**", a logical entity that effectively hides the details of very complex functions, such as managing windows, from application programs. The basic operations that are necessary for a program to conform to Apple's User Interface Standard for the Macintosh are available from the Toolbox, and all that the application must add are the highest level control structures to tie it together.

Figure 16-1 describes the components of the Toolbox and OS in a summary form. The **Memory Manager,** which is part of the OS, sets up and controls access to a region of memory known as theHeap. The **Heap** ena-

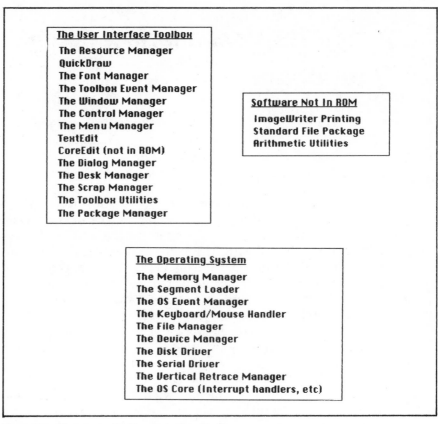

Figure 16.1   Modules in the User Interface Toolbox.

bles programs to dynamically allocate or release memory in blocks as they need it rather than claiming a large chunk when they begin executing and keeping it until they quit. Dynamic memory management allows more space-efficient usage of a given area of memory, but it does have an associated cost in execution speed. Because of the power of the 68000 processor, however, Apple felt that performance degradation would be minimal, and the Heap would allow a much more flexible user interface.

Whenever an application needs to edit text, for example, it calls **TextEdit,** which in turn calls the Memory Manager to allocate a block of memory on the Heap that will be used to store the textual data. When the edit window is closed, the block will be released, allowing another application to use the block. Any storage area that should be handled dynamically is allocated on the heap: this can include menus, resources, disk file buffers, even code for seldom-needed operations.

The other method of using memory is the **Stack,** which is used for passing parameters to and from most of the Toolbox routines. Also, Pascal procedures' local variables (the variables needed only locally within each procedure), are allocated on the Stack, and deallocated when the procedure returns to the caller. The Stack is dynamic memory in a sense, because it can grow in one direction and shrink in the other. The Stack, though, can't be cut into pieces like the Heap can; all operations on the Stack happen at one end of its current region (called the "top of stack".) It's like a pile of plates; you add and remove plates from the top of the stack (that, in fact, is why the Stack is called a stack.)

Trapping into the ROM

Most of the Toolbox routines are located in an area of memory known as the **ROM** (for Read Only Memory.) The ROM is 64K bytes long, and called from any application via a mechanism known as a Trap. Basically, a **Trap** is a special kind of instruction to the 68000 that tells it that you want to stop executing the code in your application, and begin executing somewhere else (the ROM), and then return. In Lisa Pascal, which can used to develop applications on the Lisa that run on the Macintosh, traps are handled automatically; you just call an external function that is the name of a Toolbox routine, and the Compiler and Linker set up the proper trap into the ROM. Assembly language programmers have at their disposal a set of macros that provide symbolic names for the traps.

Events

Almost any Macintosh application will be structured in a similar fashion at its highest level. Keyboard, mouse and disk actions are made known to the program via an **Event** mechanism. That is, the Operating System constantly monitors the keyboard, mouse and other peripherals, and when the user does something noteworthy with one of them, the OS makes a note of it, called an Event. It keeps a list of these notes, called the **Event Queue,** in the order that they happened. Any application that needs input from the various devices on the Mac thus becomes **Event-Driven;** this means that it has a loop at its highest level that repeatedly asks the OS what happened, and then does something about it. Remember that in most Mac applications, the user can do whatever they please with the mouse. They can select a Desk Accessory, go to the desktop and make a different window active, and so on. The application often can't require that the user enter something on the keyboard or do a particular thing with the mouse (because this would constitute a **mode.**) The exceptions to this are alert boxes, which only appear when an error of some sort has been made. Consequently, the application must be "ready for anything", and able to handle a variety of different events. The models for how this is to be done are well-established, and there are system calls to handle whatever events don't pertain directly to your application. For instance, if the user clicks the mouse in a different window from the currently active one, the application will receive what is known as a "Deactivate Event", which indicates that the current window should become inactive, and the new window should be redrawn so it is in front. The actual work of updating the window will be done by the Window manager, but the application must detect the event and call the appropriate routines.

The Dirty Work

The OS does the low-level work of managing the Macintosh hardware. It includes the primitive routines necessary to handle events, device drivers for the various I/O devices, interrupt and Trap handling, the loader that brings applications into memory when executed, and a file manager.

The Macintosh File Manager is implemented as a byte-stream system that treats files as named, ordered sequences of bytes. In this respect, the file manager bears some operational similarity to the Apple II DOS file system. The Macintosh gives a new twist to files by dividing them into two logically independent parts known as **forks.** Each file has a **resource fork,** containing the resources necessary for the file (particularly if it's an application) to be effective. It also has a **data fork,** which contains the data for the file. In an application file, the resource fork would contain both the resources and the code (which is also considered a resource for some purposes.)

Files and Volumes

iles can be considered either as continuous streams of bytes or as collections of lines separated by definable newline characters. Files are stored on **volumes,** which define a piece of storage medium by name. Volumes can be **mounted** or **unmounted,**which refers to whether they are known to the system or not; they can also be **online** or **offline,** which is related to their physical presence in a drive. Offline volumes can still be mounted; the Finder keeps information on all mounted volumes in memory. Offline files have a different appearance on the desktop to distinguish them from the files currently in the drive.

The Toolbox

The User Interface Toolbox is a set of higher-level code that calls the OS for hardware support and some software primitives. The purpose of the Toolbox is to provide an easily called library that any application developer can make use of, and to provide a powerful incentive for developing standardized applications that obey Apple's model for using the mouse, windows, menus, and other aspects of the user interface. Although some developers might choke at the thought of having to obey someone else's idea of how their application should behave, the fact remains that standardization will have a positive effect for everyone—users, Apple and third-party developers. Users will be able to learn the new applications very quickly, and developers will be able to bring up new applications without the burden of creating new user interface code each time. More resources can then be put into refining other aspects of the application, with the confidence that the user interface won't change out from under it.

Individual Toolbox Components

Let's take a closer look at the role each of the Toolbox units plays:

- The **Resource Manager** permits the separate construction and manipulation of the objects that an application works with—windows, menus, text, controls, etc. The code can be compiled separately, without the objects being defined except for general information about each one; the objects can then be created with **resource editors** or **compilers** and added to the code after linking and before loading. Then, if a change needed to be made to a menu heading, for example, it could be modified and recombined with the code instead of having to recompile the entire application. This can speed the development process greatly by isolating the user interface construction from the process of building the code. A writer or artist, for example, could build the user interface as an entirely separate process from that of the programmer who writes the code. The principal motivation for the Resource Manager was so that programs could be written that were not language-dependent (English, French, etc.) An application would store all of its text strings as resources; if it had to be converted to another language, the application would remain the same, and the resource file would be translated. This will allow the Macintosh to penetrate international markets more quickly than many machines if developers adhere to the Resource concept.

- The **Font Manager** enables an application to treat text fonts as logical entities that can be included as resources. The font specifies to the drawing package how text characters are to be built, which includes both size and stylistic variations. Several pre-defined fonts are available, in a variety of sizes; the font manager will scale an existing font if it doesn't have one in the size requested. A typical font might occupy 2-4K of disk space; consequently, fonts can represent a significant portion of an application's disk usage. The Font Mover utility enables the user to remove unneeded fonts from an application such as MacWrite and save them on a different disk.

- **QuickDraw** is in many ways the showpiece of the Macintosh software system. The Macintosh uses bit-mapped graphics to display anything on the screen, including text (see Part II for an explanation of bitmapping.) In most computers, a hardware device known as a **character generator** handles the actual generation of text on the screen. This makes it very easy to display characters, but very difficult to combine characters with drawings, because drawings must be produced by software, and must be handled in a very different fashion. Using a bitmap allows text and drawings to be treated identically; both are really just patterns of dots on the screen to the drawing software.

While powerful, bitmaps can result in a lot of conceptual and performance overhead. Since everything is done in software, performance will usually be slower than with the character generator system (at least for text.) A large body of systems software must be built that makes it easy for an application to send text and figures to the display. That's where QuickDraw comes in.

Using QuickDraw, an application can accomplish some very elaborate graphics and text display operations by using simple procedure calls. Primitives are available to manipulate points, lines, rectangles, rounded rectangles, ovals, wedges, polygons, and arbitrary "regions", or collections of points. These primitive figures can be combined, filled with definable patterns, and overlaid on each other with clipping. A drawing environment can be set up that includes several "GrafPorts", each with its own coordinate plane, set of fonts and relationship to the physical screen.

A window is easily accomplished using the GrafPort concept, defining a rectangular area of the screen that represents the "logical screen" to the application. In fact, it is QuickDraw that enables the Macintosh Desktop environment to have the graphically complex user interface that it does. The window manager, menu manager and others each call QuickDraw to accomplish their display needs.

A unique feature of QuickDraw as compared to other graphics support packages is its ability to handle "regions", which are arbitrary collections of points that needn't correspond to any given shape. Any shape can be defined as a region and then manipulated independently as a logical entity. Regions can be moved, grown or shrunk, and their intersection with any other region determined easily. Of course, the more complex the region, the more data needed to store it in memory. A rectangle is the simplest kind of region, because it requires only the X and Y locations of its upper left and lower right corners for storage.

Other important constructs in QuickDraw are the cursor, which defines the shape that the mouse pointer will take, and the pen, which determines the size and pattern of what is drawn on the screen. Both can be application-defined. The cursor automatically follows the mouse around on the screen once it is set; QuickDraw handles the drawing of the cursor in each area of the screen as you move the mouse. The pen corresponds to a given GrafPort, and has an associated height, pattern, width and location. A drawing program, for instance, could move from fine line drawing to broad brush-strokes by simply changing the pen size (as in MacPaint.) The pen and cursor are totally independent, and needn't be in the same place.

QuickDraw's most desirable feature is probably its speed. QuickDraw is fast enough that an application needn't compromise its function by doing graphics operations on its own to save time. MacPaint provides an excellent showcase for the power and speed of QuickDraw.

- The **Toolbox Event Manager** provides the application with notice of events that occur due to keyboard, mouse or disk activity. The caller can select what type of events it is interested in.

- The **Window Manager** creates, displays, moves, sizes and removes windows, and informs the application when a mouse action makes a window active or inactive. This module forms, with QuickDraw, the foundation for the "look" and functioning of the desktop. Windows present a potentially complex management problem to an application. They must be displayed correctly, including overlap with other windows. At any time the user could make a different window active, meaning that the old window has to be drawn "behind" the new one. By dragging in the title bar or size box, the user can arbitrarily change the location and dimensions of the window on the screen. Finally, whatever is displayed in the window must be appropriately "clipped", or cut off so that it can't be seen outside of the window's boundaries.

  The Window Manager does an excellent job of making this complexity manageable. The calls are at a very high level, with names like **Drag-Window, GrowWindow, SendBehind,** and **ShowWindow.** The window manager acts as an intermediary between the application and QuickDraw for the complex display operations related to windows. The kind of design work that went into the window manager makes it relatively easy for applications to achieve a common presentation style, which is Apple's avowed goal with the Macintosh software. An extensible language such as Forth can then build directly on the Toolbox calls to provide an even higher level interface for the application (see Chapter 18.)

- The **Control Manager** handles the various kinds of controls that the user can manipulate with the mouse: Buttons, check boxes, scroll bars, and so on. These items can be treated as resources, built separately from the application, and brought in and managed using the control manager. It will report when the mouse pointer is in an area that could trigger the control, and manage the display of the control according to whether it is active or inactive, visible or invisible, and so on.

- The **Menu Manager** takes most of the burden of handling pull-down menus away from the application. Menus, like many other aspects of the Macintosh desktop, can be defined separately as resources; this includes the menu bar at the top of the screen as well as the individual items on the menu. These are loaded when the application is run and made known to the menu manager. When the user presses the mouse button in the region of the menu bar, the application calls the menu manager, which then takes over and handles the tasks of pulling down individual menus and determining whether a menu item has been selected. Control then returns to the application so that it can process the menu selection.

- **TextEdit** is part of the ROM, and provides the standard editing operations **Cut, Copy** and **Paste,** as well as allowing text selection and displaying selected text properly. All text operations are performed on an **edit**

record, which links a body of textual data with a QuickDraw GrafPort so that it can be displayed. Again, the application needs to do very little to present the user with editable text that behaves in a consistent manner.

- **CoreEdit** is not part of the ROM, and adds 6K more code to an application that wishes to use it. It provides more sophisticated editing operations than TextEdit, such as justification, tabbing and the ability to display multiple character fonts and styles. CoreEdit provides a foundation for word-processing-oriented applications, doing most of the requisite dirty work.

- The **Dialog Manager** allows an application to set up dialog boxes with controls, graphics and text that behave in a standard and consistent manner. Dialogs and alerts are definable as resources, edited with a Dialog Editor or Compiler, and then brought in by the resource manager at runtime. The dialog manager calls the window manager to create and display the dialog window, and uses QuickDraw to display icons and other graphical entities.

- The **Scrap Manager** is a set of routines that handle data that's cut and pasted between applications. This data is held in the Desk Scrap, which is known to the user as the Clipboard. The Scrap can handle diverse data types including QuickDraw pictures as well as text, although some detail may be lost when the data is transferred to a different type of application. For instance, if a picture were to be transferred to a word-processing application, it is likely that the picture would have to be handled as a single unit, and individual parts of it would not be editable once it was moved to the other application.

- The **Desk Manager** allows an application to use the **Desk Accessories,** or mini-applications, that are available from the Apple menu. These are designed to be able to coexist with a running application, because they don't interfere with the currently running program's code or data. If the user selects one of the desk accessories, the application calls the desk manager to open it and handle the mouse while it is active. This is the only way in which multiple "applications" can execute concurrently on the Macintosh; normally only one can be loaded and run at a time. The desk accessories aren't really applications in the normal sense; they are implemented as I/O drivers, which means that they occupy special areas of memory that don't compete with that required by the application.

I think the Toolbox will have a very significant positive effect on how quickly good, solid software appears for the Mac. It is refreshing to have a well-researched, thoroughly tested body of code that can be relied upon to handle most interaction with the user. Any application developed with the Toolbox has a guaranteed training-time advantage because of its consistency with the standard, allowing the user to apply previously learned concepts to new applications.

On the down side, the Toolbox is big, and there is a tremendous amount to learn before one can write the simplest program using it. This would seem to be an inevitable consequence of sophistication; ironically, making things simpler for the user often makes things much harder for the developer. Many developers have overrun their schedules as a result of underestimating the commitment required to develop a Macintosh application. The initial language systems created for the Mac don't even support the Toolbox beyond QuickDraw. However, considering the power of the Macintosh desktop environment, the Toolbox is an elegant and logical consolidation into clean, manageable units of the window-based technology that is the Mac's soul. It should make possible some very sophisticated software in the next few years.

17

Pascal

A Success Story

Pascal is a language that has recently come to be accepted in both commercial and educational settings due to its readability and tendency to structure a programmer's thought process. Although poorly written code can be produced in any language, Pascal enforces a level of discipline that can reduce the number of careless mistakes that creep into programs as a result of laziness and oversight. As an indication of its level of acceptance, Pascal was recently adopted as the language for the Advanced Placement Test in Computer Science of the College Entrance Examination Board of the Educational Testing Service in Princeton, NJ.

Compilation

In Lisa Pascal, and in most Pascal environments, the programmer must use a **compiler** and **linker** to translate from the text statements that he enters with a program editor to the machine language that the computer can understand. This method is non-interactive, meaning that the programmer must save the program, tell the compiler and linker to process it, and wait. As the program gets longer, these steps require more and more time, making the process of debugging the program harder because of the time delay before it can be run. If a single mistake is made, the entire process must be repeated. This obviously can waste a lot of time, and is rather demoralizing, particularly to someone who is a little insecure with the machine to begin with.

BASIC and Interpreters

That's one of the reasons why the BASIC language became so popular as more non-technical people were exposed to computing. BASIC incorporates an editor function into the interpreter itself. This means that the program can be entered and run without intervening compilation and linking. If a statement is typed in error, the programmer finds out very quickly and can fix it without starting up a separate editor. This separates it from many of the languages that have been used for "serious" computing, such as FORTRAN and COBOL.

BASIC, however, has profound disadvantages that belie its ease of use and friendliness. BASIC, because it relies upon line numbers to express changes of control in the program (such as GOTO 1120), tends to produce hard-to-read programs that are difficult for a person unfamiliar with the code to understand. Also, BASIC makes it possible to jump around from one part of the program to another with little respect for the reader's comprehension. This technique, in the hands of a novice, can produce a program that even the author will have trouble unraveling after being away from it for awhile.

Benefits of Structured Programming

Pascal was developed by Nicolas Wirth, a proponent of **structured programming,** that is, the use of certain well-defined control structures that make it impossible to jump around indiscriminately to remote parts of the program. Structured programming forces the programmer to think about the problem in greater detail before any code is written. All variables, for instance, must be defined in Pascal **before** they are used, which minimizes the creation of variables to solve problems that would be better solved by redesign. In BASIC, variables can be created simply by using them in an expression, leading to inadvertent use of variables that have never been initialized properly with meaningful values.

Lisa Pascal

The software environments on both the Lisa and the Macintosh were designed from the ground up to use the Pascal language. Macintosh developers who started work before the release of the Mac had two choices for their target language: **Lisa Pascal** or assembly language called by a Pascal main program. Lisa Pascal is a UCSD (University of California at San Diego) standard version with a large library of routines to support the Toolbox.

Using this method, the code had to be developed on the Lisa and **downloaded** to the Macintosh via one of its serial ports. The development on the Lisa is carried out within a modified version of the **Lisa Pascal Workshop,** and the Workshop itself is somewhat difficult to use, with erratic documentation. The smallest Pascal program that can be developed under the Lisa Pascal Workshop, linked, and run on the Macintosh occupies over 6K of code because of extra information that the linker combines with the program.

This route is still the principal one taken by developers, because no alternatives have existed for serious development work until the announcement of several native Forth systems for the Macintosh (see Chapter 18.) Using the Lisa Pascal Workshop, full symbolic access to the User Interface Toolbox is provided through over 450 external procedure names. However, because of its complexity, this environment is clearly not suited for the casual user, and it requires a Lisa as its host machine.

Macintosh Pascal

To fill the gap left by conventional versions of Pascal and BASIC, **Think Technologies, Inc.,** of Danvers, Massachusetts has developed a Pascal for the Macintosh that has some very unique features. Their emphasis has been upon maximizing the interactivity and ease of use of the system to achieve a fit with Apple's expressed goals for the Macintosh. Because Apple will be marketing and distributing this package, Macintosh Pascal has had to pass inspection and meet Apple's criteria with regard to user interface standards. This should prove to be strongly in the product's favor, because it enables it to benefit from the huge research and development effort that Apple invested in the Lisa and Macintosh projects.

Traditionally, Pascal has been implemented only as a compiled language. Macintosh Pascal combines the interactivity of BASIC with the benefits of Pascal's structured approach, in a product designed to be educational as well as practical. It supports full ANSI Pascal, a standard that will ensure its compatibility with a wide variety of existing software. The basic support requires approximately 35K of the Macintosh's memory space, resulting in 45K available for user programs. THINK is also publishing a two-volume high school textbook on Macintosh Pascal that will be oriented toward the Advanced Placement Test in Computer Science.

The approach in Macintosh Pascal has been to create an **interpreter** that allows the user to build the program, test it and edit it interactively, without rigidly defined states or modes that restrict which activity can be done when. Because Pascal was designed from the ground up to be a compiled language, building an interpreter for it is hardly an easy task. An interpreter for a language such as Pascal must be much more sophisticated than one built for BASIC, because it must survive without such simplifying assumptions as line numbers. Actually, an **illusion** of interpretation must be maintained for the user, while the Pascal code is compiled in pieces and stored as machine language code. THINK Technologies appears to have done a remarkable job of achieving the functionality of standard Pascal within a truly useful interpreted environment.

Some Examples

Figure 17-1 shows an implementation in Macintosh Pascal of Euclid's algorithm for finding the greatest common divisor or two positive integers. While the code in this example is standard Pascal, the presentation format is certainly not. The Macintosh screen is divided into a number of windows that permit separate viewing of the source for the program, the user's input, and debugging information that is dynamically updated as the program executes. The window marked Euclid's Algorithm contains the tex-

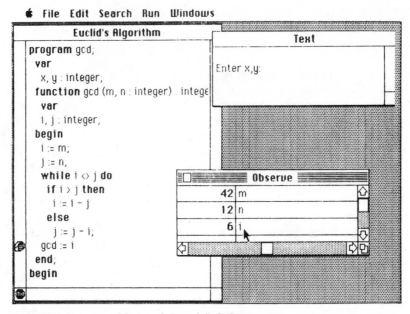

Figure 17.1 Running a Macintosh Pascal Code Segment.

tual source for the program. The indentation of program lines is accomplished automatically by the portion of the interpreter that prints listings.

The window marked **Text** is available for textual input and output relating to the executing program. It is sizeable and can be eliminated altogether if only graphical output is desired. The window marked **Observe** allows the programmer to enter the names of variables on the right side of the dividing line, and these variables will be queried and their values printed on the left side of the line as the program executes. The **Stop** sign at the bottom of the listing represents a place at which the interpreter should pause and update the information in the Observe window. This behavior is initiated by the **Go-Go** command on the **Run** menu.

Other items on the Run menu include **Step** and **Step-Step,** allowing manual and automatic line-by-line stepping through the program statements. The pointing hand denotes the statement that is currently being executed by the interpreter as it steps through the code. Using the Instant window (see Figure 17-2), while stepping through the program additional Pascal statements can be entered that query or modify the program's variables. The example shows that a routine has just been entered that calls the procedure Plink, which is being debugged. When the **Do It** button is hit, the new routine executes, and Plink is called several times with various settings of the damping conditions for an oscillator. The result is that Plink draws the curves shown in the Drawing window, which is reserved for graphics output.

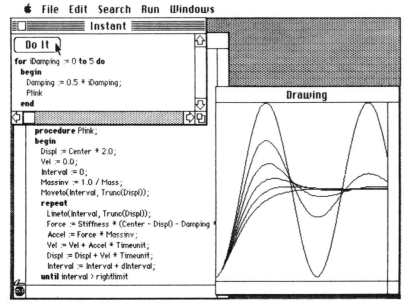

Figure 17.2   An Example of Interaction With the Program.

The implications of this ability to interact with a running program are very beneficial to the user. Instead of waiting minutes or hours for a program to be compiled and linked, you can type it in, and try it out. If it behaves differently than you had expected, you can cause it to give you more information about the source of the problem by calling it from the Instant window, and possibly displaying some variable values in the Observe window. Eventually, you will either identify the problem or isolate it to a few lines, in which case you can single-step until something wrong happens. This drastically reduces the overall time required to identify a problem and correct.

There is another aspect to the interpreter-based design that makes it especially valuable in an educational setting. Because program editing facilities are so readily available, it becomes practical to take any piece of code and experiment with it, quickly being able to see the results of any changes that you have made. This leads to an understanding of the program that cannot be achieved by treating it as a passive object, only to be observed. The best way to learn any language is by using it, and there is no better way to use a language than actively interacting with it in the manner of Macintosh Pascal.

QuickDraw Interface

In Figure 17-3 we see a program segment that is intended to fit a line to a curve using least-squares analysis. The user plots points by clicking with the mouse, and then the program responds by computing the line that best

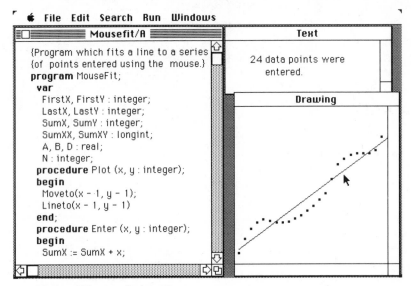

17.3 Fitting a Line to a Series of Points.

fits the curve, meaning that its average deviation from the curve over its entire length is minimized with respect to other lines that could be drawn. The procedures Moveto() and Lineto() are examples of how Macintosh Pascal interfaces with the Toolbox routines. The names of these routines are very close to those used by Lisa Pascal. Unfortunately, beyond the QuickDraw routines, there is very little support for the rest of the Toolbox, such as the Window Manager, Menu Manager, and so on. The emphasis is on creating programs that run within the window and menu structure set up by Macintosh Pascal, and not defining new ones. Memory limitations in the 128K Macintosh restrict severely the amount of Toolbox support that a language can provide, unless it is highly compact in the manner of Forth.

While this s suitable for educational use, it certainly doesn't meet the needs of developers, or even users who wish to write their own applications. As long as an application could be built that required no menu support, this system could be used; but that contravenes the very philosophy that Apple has so strongly promoted. THINK Technologies has announced a set of **Developer's Tools** that will provide more complete Toolbox support, and will support the division of a program into **modules,** smaller pieces that apparently will be separately loadable and can be reused in other applications. This is very important in an environment in which the same sorts of things must be done in every application, as is the case with the Mac user interface. The developer can then discard the development support, such as the debugger and editor, before the program is run to minimize space. Release is slated for second quarter of 1984.

Figure 17-4 shows another program that makes use of QuickDraw to draw a series of circles. The QuickDraw procedure FrameOval draws an oval outline inside any specified rectangle. If the rectangle is square, a

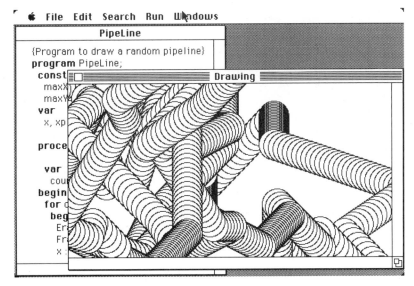

17.4 Drawing Circles with QuickDraw.

circle will result. In this program, the circles are drawn on a random series of connected line segments, resulting in a "pipeline" effect. Drawing that occurs outside the boundaries of the window is clipped, and doesn't result in an error condition. Other QuickDraw routines are available to erase ovals, fill them with patterns, and invert the color of each dot int he oval. These operations can also be applied to the other primitives that QuickDraw makes available, including rectangles, polygons, rounded rectangles, and regions.

Summary

Macintosh Pascal is a very nicely designed package which should generate a tremendous amount of interest from the educational community. It is also quite suitable for the home user who would like to learn Pascal but has previously been intimidated by it. There can be no comparison between the interpreted approach and the traditional compile-link-run system for ease of use and friendliness. Macintosh Pascal hasn't been targeted for the serious business user, and probably won't be very useful for that group until the full-blown development system is available. Until then, developers will have to either broach the esoteric confines of Forth or settle for the Lisa Pascal Workshop and its attendant drawbacks.

18

BASIC and Forth

Microsoft Basic

Microsoft, undeniably the world's most prolific producers of microcomputer BASICs, had a jump on the rest of the software development world due to their early involvement in the Macintosh project. They worked closely with Apple starting more than a year before the Mac was announced, both contributing to the design of some systems software and converting their version of BASIC to run on the Mac and make use of its unique environment. As a result, Microsoft BASIC was the only native language running on the Macintosh at its release.

For previous users of MS-BASIC, this version will not be a surprise in most respects. All of the standard commands are there, and most programs written in MS-BASIC should run on the Mac with little or no change. MS-BASIC has evolved over the years from the CP/M version, which has no graphics or sound commands, to the versions created for the IBM PC and other more recent machines, which do include graphics, sound and other more sophisticated features. The Mac version shares much of its statement syntax with those in the latter group, especially the PC version.

One question that will be asked of every language product that runs on the Mac is how fully it supports the User Interface Toolbox, providing access to the Window Manager, the Menu Manager, and so on. Microsoft has chosen to support a small part of the Toolbox in terms of the language itself, providing access only to a portion of the QuickDraw routines for graphics operations. Even that interface is rather indirect, not supported directly by BASIC statements, but with a generalized CALL instruction. This will certainly disappoint someone who was hoping to take advantage of the power of the Toolbox, but will most likely not be missed by novices in the programming process.

The bottom line is that this product was not really intended for serious applications development on the Macintosh, because it doesn't provide the support needed to conform to the User Interface Guidelines that Apple is promoting. Rather, MS-BASIC is a good instructional tool that can do some things very easily, and provides a framework for programs written for other systems to work on the Mac. This framework provides a single "output window" that simulates the screen on a conventional computer or terminal, and within this window, standard screen formatting commands function normally.

Figure 18-1 shows the MS-BASIC screen with a simple one-line program entered into the program area. At the bottom of the screen is a window marked "Command." This window is highlighted and pops up to the front

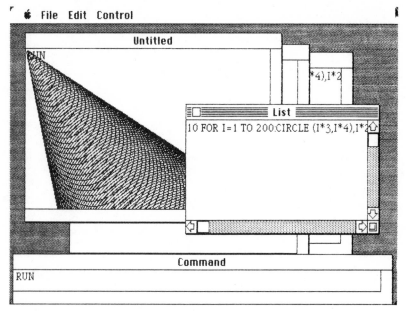

Figure 18.1   The MS-BASIC Screen.

whenever you enter anything at the keyboard. Its purpose is to indicate that BASIC is ready to accept a command, just as the "OK" prompt does in other BASICs. When you type a command, the characters are echoed in the Command window until you hit Return, at which time they are accepted by the interpreter and printed in the output window (marked "Untitled.")

The window marked "List" displays a listing of the program whenever you type the List command into the Command window, or select List on the Control menu. Up to three List windows can be active simultaneously, and they will simply propagate if you type successive List commands. The other two partially obscured windows in the illustration are both List windows. Only the List window has scroll bars, because that is the only window in which anything can be edited after it is entered. To add lines to the program, you enter them with appropriate line numbers into the Command window. When you hit return on a line with a preceding number, the line will then appear in both he output and the List windows.

After the novelty of the MS-BASIC window arrangement wears off, it has some aspects that are rather disappointing. One problem is that the windows jump around a lot, depending on what you've just done. Because the Toolbox requires that a window which is to display something must also be in front and highlighted, as soon as you enter a command, such as LIST, the various windows start bouncing around as text is displayed in each of them. This can be rather disconcerting if you're not used to it, and is also slow. And, if you happen to be looking at a List window, but the Command window is lurking somewhere behind it, the first key you type will cause the Command window to jump to the front and obscure the List. Always having three List windows around, which is pretty much inevitable, leads to a vague sense of confusion about what is in the hidden windows, and can be distracting.

None of these problems are debilitating, they just aren't very pretty. A missing feature that seems to be a major oversight is the ability to Cut and Paste from the output window to the Command window. Imagine for a moment that you have just entered a lengthy command into the Command window, because you are testing a graphics statement to see how it should be constructed. As soon as you hit the Return key, the text that you typed was placed in the output window and executed. If it worked, it would be extremely convenient to be able to point to the text in the output window with the mouse, and then Copy or Cut it to the Clipboard and Paste it into the Command window again, at which point you need only add a line number. Sadly, fine points like this, which have been so tirelessly refined in Apple's and Microsoft's applications, seem to be absent from MS-BASIC.

It would appear that the person who wrote the manual that comes with MS-BASIC also had some of these nonexistent functions in mind. On page 21, mention is made of cutting and pasting between List windows; unfortunately, you can't do that; you can only Cut and Paste in the Command window. Hopefully, these obvious flaws in an otherwise useful product will be corrected before version 1.1 of MS-BASIC is released.

The menus available in MS-BASIC are **File,** which performs the obvious Get and Save functions, **Edit,** providing Cut and Paste for the Command window only, and **Control,** providing access via mouse to some of the standard BASIC control statements, such as Stop, List, Trace On/Off, and so on.

When you select **Open** on the File menu, you are prompted to enter the filename in a dialog (see Figure 18-2.) Unfortunately, this isn't the standard Open dialog that other applications use, which lists all of the files on the disk appropriate for the application and allows one to be selected with the mouse rather than entering the name. The manual seems to imply that the latter method is used, but it's not. Also, nowhere in MS-BASIC did I find a way to eject the disk. In other words, if the file you want is on a different disk, you have to exit BASIC completely, eject the disk, insert the new one, and start BASIC again. This is a real problem, and again points out that something was missing in the design and testing process.

The **Save** command from the File menu offers three formats for the saved file: ASCII, Binary, and Protected. **ASCII** saves the file as text in a format that could be used with word processors and other text-handling

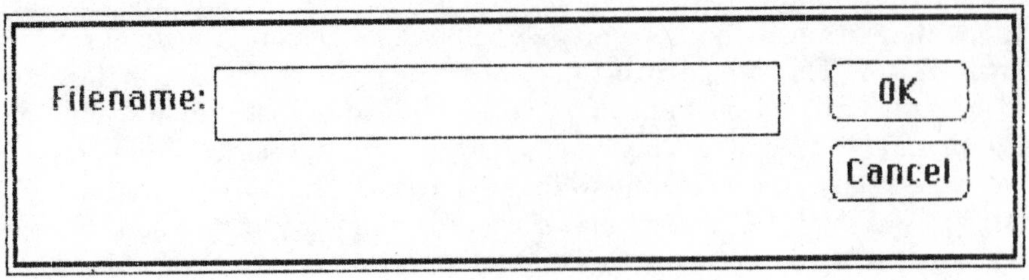

Figure 18.2   The LOAD file dialog.

Figure 18.3   The SAVE file dialog.

applications. **Binary** is the default, and results in faster loading and saving because it is much more compact. **Protected** disables the ability to List or Edit the program, useful for applications that will be distributed commercially.

The Edit window contains the three basic commands Cut, Copy and Paste. Since these are only applicable to the Command window, and it can hold at most a single command line, their utility is severely compromised. Since a program may read or write to the Clipboard as if it were a file, some interesting uses could probably be found for Cut and Paste inside a program.

The Control menu contains Stop, which enables you to stop a running application; Continue, which may be used to resume after a Stop; Suspend, which waits for a key to be pressed before continuing; List, Run and Trace On/Off. This is an adequate set of control commands, but other features could certainly be added that would enhance the utility of the package. One would be a debug window, that displays debug information such as variable values in a separate window while the program is running so as not to disturb the program's normal output. This area is where MacPascal really excells. If BASIC permitted you to define user windows, you could fake it, but this is not the case.

At the statement level, this BASIC is very close to Microsoft's BASIC for the IBM PC. In several areas, these two BASIC's have been similarly extended past the usual MS-BASIC statement set. The LINE command draws a line or box between two points, expressed as either relative or absolute locations. CIRCLE draws oval shapes with size and aspect ratio determined by the user. Both circles and boxes can be filled with either black or white.

GET and PUT provide the ability to store graphics points in an array and later retrieve them, placing them within a designated rectangle on the screen. This includes resizing the image to fit the target rectangle, a facility that QuickDraw provides and BASIC exploits. The MOUSE function returns parameters that relate to the current state of the mouse. The mouse's current location, whether its button has been pressed, and its location before and after a drag operation are available from this function.

Double precision arithmetic, up to 14 digits, is standard with this BASIC, due mostly to the large register size of the 68000. A **Decimal Math Package** provides 14-digit decimal precision for financial applications, and minimizes rounding error, a source of difficulty in some BASICs.

MS-BASIC provides a **device-independent** I/O facility on the Macintosh. This means that you can treat any of the Input/Output devices on the Mac in the same way from the point of view of the program. Available devices include the output window, the keyboard, the printer, the Clipboard, and the communications port. Macintosh BASIC has no ability to set the communications parameters for the port, such as baud rate, parity, and the like. This contrasts poorly with IBM PC BASIC, which provides an excellent facility for specifying these parameters when the port is opened.

File names on the Macintosh can be up to 255 characters in length, including numbers and spaces. BASIC reflects this, although the dialog boxes permit far fewer than 255 characters. BASIC uses no automatic extensions such as ".BAS", but the user is free to use any extensions that are desired.

There is no support in MS-BASIC for the Macintosh's excellent sound capability, other than a BEEP word that emits a single beep of fixed frequency. Again, this is disappointing. It is somewhat understandable owing to the complexity of the software required to support full sound capability. It seems likely that more sound capability will be added in a future release.

Figure 18-4 shows a sample program that is distributed by Microsoft with the BASIC software. To edit a listing, a line can be selected and moved into the Command window by double-clicking on it with the mouse. You can then use the mouse and keyboard as you would on any text in a Mac application. This sample begins by setting up an integer array of 1025 elements called A in line 110. Line 120 executes the subroutine at 220 which draws the picture. Since we can't see that part of the listing, we can enter another List command and get a second List window (see Figure 18-5.) The subroutine at 220 clears the screen, draws the black box with a LINE statement, and draws a series of circles inside the box with lines

260-290. This is done only once, to get the picture up on the screen; after
that, it will be moved with GET and PUT statements.

The subroutine returns to line 130, where it copies the current picture
into the array A. Lines 150-170 test the mouse, to determine if it has moved
more than a few dots; if so, the picture is re-drawn over itself to erase it, and

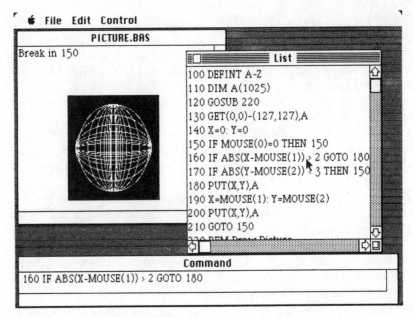

Figure 18.4   A Sample MS-BASIC Program.

then drawn in the new mouse position. Line 210 jumps back to 150, and the
process is begun again. The net result is that the picture follows the mouse
around on the screen as long as the button is down. If the mouse is dragged,
rather severe flickering occurs, because BASIC is unable to redraw the
image faster than 30 times per second, which is the threshold at which we
notice visual change.

Figure 18-6 summarizes the results of running four benchmark programs written in MS-BASIC on both the Macintosh and the IBM PC. Identical programs were run on both machines. The first was a simple loop: FOR
I=1 TO 30000:A=B:NEXT. This tests the raw speed of a basic control
structure in the interpreter. The second test created 200 circles on the
screen with size determined by an index in a loop. This compares the speed
of the graphics primitives in each case. The third benchmark did a string
assignment from one 80-character string to another 10,000 times. The last
routine printed the word "Macintosh" on the screen with a carriage return
1000 times.

In general, MS-BASIC on the Macintosh seems to be 30 to 40 percent
faster than its IBM PC equivalent. This owes principally to the power of the

68000 cpu versus the PC's 8088. The second benchmark was 50 percent faster on the Macintosh, which demonstrates the additional performance advantage provided by the highly optimized QuickDraw code over the PC's less optimized graphics routines.

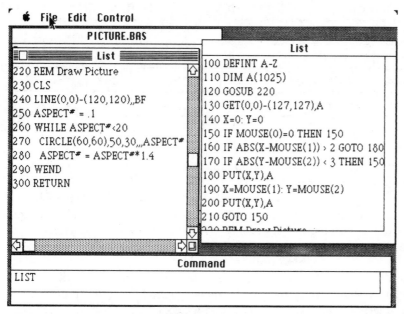

Figure 18.5 Using Two List Windows.

In terms of memory usage, I tried using the FRE(n) function to determine how much space was available for user programs and data. FRE(-1) returns the number of bytes in the heap that are available, and FRE(1) returns the number of free bytes in BASIC's memory space. Unfortunately, no mention is made of what goes in the heap and what goes in the memory space; I would venture a guess that string storage, among other items, occupies the heap. In any case, without a loaded program, there are 14042 bytes available on the heap and 14968 in memory space, for a grand total of 28K on a 128K Mac. That's not a heck of a lot for serious programming, and it indicates why so many Macintosh-specific functions seem to be missing from this BASIC. There wasn't room to add any functionality and still have a usable memory area.

The documentation for BASIC could use a more complete section explaining how this BASIC works on the Macintosh. Much of the reference section of the manual was obviously inherited from previous versions of MS-BASIC. Many excellent examples highlight individual statement explanations, which is a very appealing feature. While this manual is superior to its predecessors in the BASIC genre, I don't think it meets the standards that Microsoft set for itself with its Macintosh Multiplan documentation.

In summary, if you're relatively new to programming, and want to learn BASIC on the Macintosh, or if you have some simple programs in Microsoft BASIC that you would like to use on the Mac, this BASIC will be useful. If

Benchmark	Macintosh BASIC	IBM PC BASIC
1. For/Next * 30000	0:43	1:01
2. 200 Circles	0:24	0:52
3. 10000 String Moves	0:28	0:40
4. 1000 PRINTs	1:13	1:54

Figure 18.6   Results of the Benchmark Tests.

you're considering serious development on the Mac, I think you'll find MS-BASIC frustrating in its failure to exploit the Macintosh's power. Its user interface leaves much to be desired when compared to other Macintosh applications, but easily outstrips most previous MS-BASIC implementations because of the mouse. If Microsoft pays attention to the public's assessment of their product, as they usually do, future versions of MS-BASIC could be considerably improved.

Apple's version of BASIC for the Macintosh, MacBASIC, will support some areas of the Toolbox, but will also be intended for educational rather than production use. MacBasic will produce code that is much more readable than other BASICS. Among its advantages will be the use of labels for lines instead of line numbers, and Toolbox calls that are easily read, such as **Set PenMode 6.**)

Forth

Few languages are so controversially discussed or as poorly understood as Forth. Its critics campaign loudly against its obscurity and arcane syntax, while Forth's proponents proclaim its speed, compactness and raw power. Until the BYTE issue of August, 1980 that was devoted to Forth, few people even knew what it was. Since that time, the Forth community has steadily grown, and now microcomuter software developers are beginning to embrace Forth for its undeniable speed and size advantages.

I have used Forth personally and professionally for several years, and have experience bothits advantages and its problems. At Kriya Systems, Inc. we have used Forth for some time as our exclusive development language. Among several mass-market products that we have used Forth to implement is the highly successful **Typing Tutor III with Letter Invaders™ program,** which at one point was implemented in compiled Microsoft BASIC and occupied over 200K in four object modules. When implemented PC/Forth from Laboratory Microsystems, Inc., this product required only a single object that was 48K long, and ran three to five times as fast.

Forth's problems are inseparable from its power. A programmer can literally do anything with Forth, including destroy the operating system or user program. Very little protection is built into Forth, but a lot of flexibility is, so that an environment can be constructed in which the programmer is prevented from making fatal mistakes. This requires adding on to the basic Forth system, which is relatively easy, because Forth is an extensible language. Extensibility means that the programmer is free to modify the way that the Forth interpreter/compiler itself behaves, and thereby add to the language and even make Forth into a different language! As a demonstration of this, Charles Moore, the inventor of Forth, once implemented a Tiny BASIC compiler in a couple of pages of Forth code. He did it by modifying Forth itself to read and behave like BASIC, not a desirable thing in itself, but useful as a demonstration.

To write good Forth code, programmers must exercise a lot of discipline in the design and coding process. The discipline involves breaking a problem down into very small, functionally clear pieces in the manner of traditional top-down design, and choosing clear and readable names for those pieces when they are implemented in Forth. Given this discipline, we have found Forth's advantages to far outweigh its drawbacks, because it makes things possible that would otherwise be unattainable on personal computers.

A phenomenon that has worked in Forth's behavior has been the propensity of Forth programmers for publishing a lot of their code and ideas in the public domain. This has occurred largely through the efforts of the Forth Interest Group, and is unparalleled in the history of modern computing languages. FIG distributes for a nominal fee the information necessary to implement Forth on nearly every microprocessor ever developed, and Forth vendors such as Laboratory Microsystems sell more sophisticated and optimized versions at reasonable prices. It is largely through the efforts of these vendors that have chosen to keep prices reasonable and information free that Forth has become much more widely used in the last few years. A few vendors have pursued policies of high prices and nondisclosure of source code, but they are by far in the minority.

Because of this phenomenon, Forth often appears very quickly on a new machine, usually long before more conventional language systems are converted. Such has been the case with the Macintosh. Creative Solutions, Inc. released its MacForth product in the first quarter of 1984, and other vendors are rumored to be close to releasing products as well. We at Kriya Systems have chosen to implement our own version of Forth for internal development use on the Macintosh, with considerable help from Ray Duncan at Laboratory Microsystems.

The irony is that these Forth systems represented the only serious development tools that were native to the Macintosh in the first several months after its release. By the time this book is published, other means of development on the Mac could be available, but as of the first quarter of 1984, only Think Technologies' Pascal was slated for expansion into a full-blown development system, and it wasn't to be available until summer of 1984. Apple has no plans to move the Lisa Pascal Workshop to the Macintosh for the immediate future.

A typical Macintosh Forth system will have between 40K and 60k available for user code, which goes a long way in Forth. In our system, we have chosen to extend Forth in the direction of **object-oriented languages** such as Simula and Smalltalk, because this approach fits in nicely with the User Interface Guidelines and the Toolbox design that shape Macintosh applications. Object-oriented languages deal with **objects and classes** rather than variables and functions and procedures. Objects possess the ability to process **messages** which request particular functions, and they possess a **local data area** upon which the functions can operate. The specifics of how the functions are carried out are known only to the receiving object, and are hidden from the sender.

Objects can be built from other objects, and aggregated to reflect the structure of some part of the problem. Objects having common characteristics are grouped into **classes,** and classes can spawn subclasses that elaborate on the characteristics of their parent class. By this method, the program becomes a direct mapping of the structure of the behavior that is being simulated.

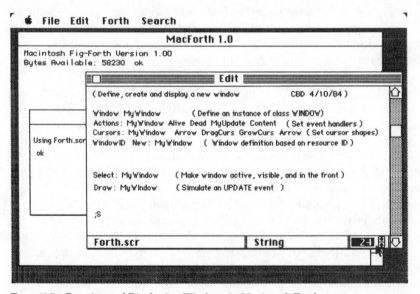

Figure 18.7   Creating and Displaying Windows in Macintosh Forth.

In the case of the Macintosh, a meaningful candidate for a class is the window. To create a new window, the programmer creates an object of class Window, initializes it, and sends it messages to show itself, highlight, disappear, and so on. Figure 18-7 gives an example of how source to create and display a window would look in our Forth system. The process of defining classes and objects can be continued arbitrarily, eventually comprising the entire application. We have found that source code using this approach is highly readable and self-documenting, which is extremely important when using Forth. Support for the entire Toolbox can be built from these structures, so the user isn't locked into a static level of support.

For the sake of comparison, I coded the BASIC benchmarks from the last chapter in Forth on both the PC and the Macintosh. Speeds were from 3 to 15 times faster using Forth, as summarized in Figure 18-8. Given the dearth of alternatives, Forth on the Macintosh may prove to be a solution for a lot of developers and casual users, and the language may finally get some of the attention that it deserves. For more information on Forth, contact: Forth Interest Group, PO BOX 1105, San Carlos, CA 94070.

Benchmark	Macintosh BASIC	Macintosh Forth
1. For/Next * 30000	0:43	0:03
2. 200 Circles	0:24	0:09
3. 10000 String Moves	0:28	0:08
4. 1000 PRINTs	1:13	0:43

Figure 18.8 Results of the Benchmarks Using Macintosh Forth.

Macintosh BASIC

Apple's **Macintosh BASIC** has a variety of attractive features that set it widely apart from previous implementations. This BASIC was developed expressly for the Macintosh, and as such exploits many attributes unique to that machine. In addition to the QuickDraw support found in other language systems, Macintosh BASIC allows the programmer to create windows, menus and dialogs as components of the program's user interface. Thus, new applications can be created hat are reasonably consistent with Apple's User Interface Guidelines.

This BASIC uses incremental compilation to create code that executes much faster than standard interpreted code. When a line is entered, a preliminary syntax check is made immediately; many typing mistakes and faulty keywords will be caught as the line is entered. If it passes, the line is converted to **B-Code,** which is an intermediate language between BASIC and the machine language understood by the CPU. This B-Code is later interpreted when the program is run, and converted to machine language instructions.

The editor in this system includes a Search function, generally not found in BASIC editors. You can have the system automatically find all occurrences of a certain character sequence, and optionally change them to a different string. Programs can be saved either as text files, modifiable by anyone, or B-Code files that cannot be examined or changed.

Toward a Structured BASIC

Perhaps the most significant characteristic of this BASIC is its improvement on the usual BASIC control structures. IF/THEN/ELSE structures, which must occupy a single line in other versions, can run over several lines. Line numbers are not mandatory, and meaningful labels can be assigned to points in the code. SELECT CASE/ENDSELECT is an extremely useful structure that all by itself will go a long way toward making programs readable. The net result of these improvements is a structured language that overcomes most of traditional BASIC's control deficiencies. The drawback is a lack of compatibility with other versions, but this might be a blessing in disguise.

Debug

An interactive **Debug** feature makes good use of the mouse and windows to single-step a program, display its variables during execution, and allow modification of source to correct problems. Breakpoints can be tied to the value of a variable; when the value falls within a certain range, the program pauses and displays its status. This is often the fastest way to determine why a program is failing, and is often left out of debugging tools in other systems. A commented alphabetical listing of the program's labels is available in a separate window, providing excellent documentation to accompany comments embedded in the code.

Graphics are well supported with a variety of calls to QuickDraw (such as Frame Oval), and commands to save and recall a graphics picture saved in a picture array. ROTATE, SCALE and ANIMATE provide the ability to easily manipulate a graphics image and create dynamic displays. An Output window holds both graphical and textual output generated by the program.

Macintosh BASIC should be a welcome addition to the programming language library for the Mac, both for its intelligent extension of standard BASIC syntax and its use of Macintosh-specific features to provide a friendlier, more powerful language. It is scheduled for release in the summer of 1984.

Appendices

Appendix A covers the historical lineage of the Macintosh,
beginning with work done by Alan Kay and the Learning
Research Group at Xerox PARC which produced the
Smalltalk language. Apple's Lisa project inherited much of its
philosophical underpinnings from this work, and in turn molded
the design of the Macintosh. Appendix B is a comparison
of the Macintosh versus the IBM PC in a variety of areas
that would be relevant to someone considering a purchase.

A Brief History of Desktop Computing

Dynabook

In late 1977, Dr. Alan C. Kay, then of Xerox Palo Alto Research Center (PARC), wrote, "Ideally, the personal computer will be designed in such a way that people of all ages and walks of life can mold and channel its power to their own needs... If the computer is to be truly "personal", adult and child users must be able to get it to perform useful activities without resorting to the services of an expert. Simple tasks must be simple, and complex ones must be possible" (Reference 1.) At that time, the personal computer was little more than a concept, although relatively inexpensive, hobbyist-oriented hardware in such forms as the Altair and the Apple I had appeared.

In his 1977 paper in Scientific American, Dr. Kay described his far-reaching vision of a machine which, although notebook-sized, would contain mass storage, high-resolution bitmapped graphics, and powerful software oriented toward the simulation of real-world phenomena. He saw this machine as being a universal tool that could simulate, or look and act like, something that was within a person's field of endeavor, be it architecture, music, or auto mechanics. This machine, code named Dynabook, could only be approximated in 1977 because the software required hardware that was necessarily much larger than the envisioned handheld package.

Kay's work at Xerox PARC, although it never directly resulted in a manifestation of his vision, set the stage for some of the most exciting developments in today's personal computer field, including the basis for the technology in Apple's Lisa and Macintosh machines. Let's back up for a moment and take a look at some of the people and ideas that preceded Kay's important paper, and who began the history of so-called "desktop" computing.

Simula and Flex

In the mid-1960's, Ole-Johan Dahl and Kristen Nygaard of the Norwegian Computing Center in Oslo developed a language called Simula. In contrast to other languages, such as Fortran, that were oriented toward scientific calculation, Simula was specifically built to create computer programs that could model real-world phenomena. The most interesting contribution of Simula was its tractability—programs could be written in Simula that were close to the natural language of the problem, as opposed to the more obscure, hard-to-understand programs that resulted with conventional languages.

Alan Kay and Edward Cheadle collaborated in the late 1960's on a personal computer that directly supported a graphics and simulation-oriented language. This system, developed at the University of Utah, was called **FLEX,** and its chief emphasis was on simplicity and ease of use. Kay based the FLEX software upon the more attractive features of Simula, having come to the conclusion that simulation was the central purpose of the ideal personal computer. The justification for this was that a computer that was built for simulation could look and act in a more familiar manner, and therefore be more easily learned by an unskilled person.

The hardware that supported FLEX was far too expensive in the 1960s to be truly "personal", and the software environment was, in Kay's words, "not comprehensive enough to be useful to a wide variety of nonexpert users" (Reference 1.) FLEX was significant in that it began to concretize what was then a radical notion of a computer that could be used in every-day activities by individuals of age six and above, could be transported easily, and was built for simulation.

The Mouse is Born

At the same time, Douglas Englebart was working at Stanford Research Institute on a project whose goal was the augmentation of human intellect via computers. This rather lofty endeavor produced two innovations that greatly influenced the work of Alan Kay and others. One was the **mouse,** a box with wheels on the bottom that was electronically linked to a pointer on the screen of a terminal. Pointing was recognized early on in computer system design as a desirable alternative to the keyboard, being much more direct and unambiguous. Light pens had already enabled people to point to a place on the screen and have the computer recognize it, but they had the disadvantage of losing their place when put down. The process of leaving the keyboard, picking up the light pen, and pointing was disruptive and could tire the user's arm if done frequently enough. The mouse stayed put when not being used, and was no more tiresome than using the keyboard. It was also fairly inexpensive to manufacture, and Englebart's studies had shown it to be a superior method from the standpoint of productivity (Reference 2.)

Windows

Englebart's second innovation was the use of **windows,** which divided up the screen into rectangular sections that could hold different pieces of information. The user could point to a section of a window with the mouse in order to perform operations on it such as Insert, Delete and Move for editing text. This system utilized two important postulates about how people work with computers: The first is that people often require several kinds of information in **parallel,** or simultaneously, in order to do their work efficiently. This might involve several completely different groups of information, or just different ways of organizing the same information (e.g., alphabetically versus chronologically.) Secondly, that it is much easier to point to something on the screen than it is to specify it with a series of keystrokes; pointing allows the **direct manipulation** of objects on the screen as opposed to indirect specification via the keyboard. These principles, as we shall see later, were extremely important in the development of the desktop metaphor.

PARC and the Creation of Smalltalk

In 1971, Dr. Kay moved to Xerox PARC and founded the Learning Research Group as a vehicle for research and development on the Dynabook project. Although Dynabook was conceived as a personal machine for the 80's, prototype implementations would be created on intermediate hardware as it became smaller and more available. Kay came armed with three major concepts in his attack on the elusive personal computer: the philosophy of ease of use and tractability behind Simula and FLEX, windows as display media, and the mouse as the preferred general-purpose input device. He began exploring ways that the personal computer could utilize a "physical metaphor", meaning that it could look and act like familiar objects in our everyday world, and therefore be easily learned by applying one's intuition. The **Smalltalk** language was created shortly after the founding of LRG, and was intended to be the software environment for this work.

Better Windows

Kay had developed the concept of **overlapping windows** as a response to what Dan Swinehart termed the **preemption dilemma** (Reference 3.) In many computer systems, running a program effectively takes over the system and disallows you from using other facilities of the system, thereby setting up a **"mode"** and obscuring the work at hand (Reference 3.) This is true even today in many systems, an indication that the solution to this problem is not a trivial one. For instance, while composing a memo, it might be desirable to see sales figures in another part of the screen; on many current systems, using the word processor would preempt the use of any other programs, such as spreadsheets. Englebart's work had shown windows to be an effective improvement upon the single screen mode because they allowed parallel activities on the same screen, and therefore reduced the preemption problem. In the SRI model, the windows were predefined, fixed, non-overlapping areas on the screen, not alterable by the user (Reference 4).

Kay's paradigm improved upon the scheme developed at SRI by using **overlapping windows,** meaning that only one of the rectangles was "on top", or completely visible, at any given time, and this window could overlap and partially obscure the others. Thus, the windows exist in planes that have a spatial depth from the viewer. They are able to represent more information, just as a stack of papers contains more information than a single sheet. Windows function most effectively in conjunction with a pointing device, because then the user can simply point to a given window and it becomes completely visible. If the windows can be moved around, the information that they contain can be positioned in such a way as to be most useful to the viewer; these early windows, however, were not movable, but were fixed in position by the program.

Kay saw windows and the mouse as essential to his ultimate personal computer because of the need for simultaneity and parallelism in a tool of this type (Reference 3.) He saw that people are accustomed to thinking of several things at one time as they do their work, switching between them as circumstances dictate. The next problem was to develop the suitable hardware to test some of these new ideas.

Alto—A Personal Graphics Machine

Xerox began development of the Alto computer system around this time, intending it to be a personal research machine that could support some of the concepts being developed by LRG. Alto was the first "personal" computer to incorporate a really powerful **bitmapped display.** This type of display is set up as a grid of dots, so tiny that they are virtually indistinguishable. Each dot is either on, (producing light), or off (dark.) In the bitmap, all kinds of information, whether text or graphics objects such as rectangles and circles, are treated as groupings of these dots and must be produced by software. In non-bitmapped systems, text is generally produced by a hardware device, and its style and size cannot be easily modified (see Figure A-1.) Bitmaps provide the ultimate in flexibility, since any kind of image can be built up from the dots (also known as bits or pixels.) Text can be represented in a variety of fonts, styles and sizes, limited only by the flexibility of the software.

The drawback is that the usual bitmapped display relies upon software to do its work, which can slow down the operation of other programs that are running on the machine. Because of this, bitmapped systems need to incorporate either very powerful main processors or extremely efficient systems software in order to be fast enough for convenient use. Also, a lot of expensive, fast memory is needed to store the screen information. A bitmapped display is a prerequisite for any system using a mouse and windows, since these systems are highly visual and need to draw the rectangles for windows and pointer shapes for the mouse at arbitrary positions on the screen. Expense has been a major reason why bitmapped displays haven't been seen in more personal computer systems to date; with memory prices dropping precipitously, many more of these systems have recently appeared on the market.

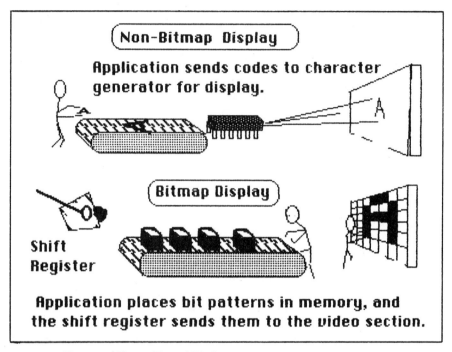

Figure A.1   Bitmapped Versus Normal Displays.

Alto came in at approximately $30,000, and was never commercially available. It was built entirely for research, and distributed mostly to universities and within Xerox (Reference 5.) Alto used a mouse with three buttons on the top and ran a window-based operating system and a text editor called Bravo, which was controlled by a combination of mouse and keyboard commands. The mouse required a special piece of plastic underneath it which had fine lines that were optically detected to determine changes in position. Most Altos were loaded with between 256,000 and 512,000 bytes, which in the early 1970's was truly a lot of memory, and contributed toward a large portion of the cost.

The **Bravo text editor** is worthy of note, because it was the first major implementation of a "what-you-see-is-what-you-get" editor (Reference 6.) Bravo used the versatility of the bitmap to present a very accurate image on the screen of what a document would actually look like when printed, including various text fonts and sizes. Bravo did have its drawbacks, particularly in its use of "modes", which we will discuss later in this chapter.

Another program that had an impact on later developments was the **Draw** program, which enabled the user to draw pictures and paint with electronic "brushes" on the bitmapped display. Some features of Draw had an obvious influence on the design of the **MacPaint** application on the Macintosh.

Smalltalk

The Alto provided Kay's LRG with a machine on which to prototype the Dynabook. In 1972, LRG designed and implemented the first version of the **Smalltalk** language to provide a foundation for the Dynabook software. Smalltalk, like FLEX, was deeply influenced by the concepts in Simula, and was designed to be a powerful, yet simple, programming environment enabling people of all ages to mold Dynabook to their individual needs. Its philosophical basis was that a small set of principles could be applied consistently to build more complex systems, and this process could be continued indefinitely (Reference 1.) The development of Smalltalk probably contributed more than any other single phenomenon to what is today known as the desktop environment. Smalltalk was born of a desire for power within simplicity, and this philosophy was to extend not only throughout the design of the language, but into the user interface as well.

Modes

In 1973, Larry Tesler joined LRG and began to mount an attack on the preemption dilemma and the use of "modes" in software design. He defined modes as artificial states created by a program solely for the purpose of placing an interpretation on user input. For instance, some text editors have a switchable "Insert Mode", within which any characters that you type will be inserted between existing characters in the document. If you leave Insert Mode, the characters you type will **replace** existing characters. Going back and forth between modes can be confusing and often maddening, because you're never quite sure what the computer is going to do next.

Tesler set to work at LRG, hoping to banish modes forever from the design of interactive office systems (Reference 3.) This work resulted in a paradigm for user interface design that was incorporated into the Smalltalk system by Dan Ingalls in 1976, and, in a more evolved form, into the Lisa Office System in 1981 (Reference 7.) Tesler's model makes extensive use of the mouse, taking advantage of the positive, unambiguous nature of pointing to objects on the screen. His basic ground rules were: 1) **Selection precedes command.** The user moves the mouse to the object, whether image or text, that he wishes to select, and then uses the mouse buttons to select it. He or she is then able to choose from a set of applicable commands, based upon the nature of the object that was selected. No ambiguity is possible, and only appropriate commands are shown to the user. 2) **Typing text replaces the selection.** The selection is shown with a black border around it, and if a character is typed after the selection is made, it replaces the selection. Typing text characters never produces a command. This behavior is adhered to throughout the interface.

Commands are chosen in the Smalltalk-76 interface via **pop-up menus.** A special button on the three-button mouse is devoted to producing these menus, which comprise a list of command choices within a box on the screen, whenever the button is pressed. The mouse pointer can then be moved to the desired command, and the button released to choose the command. Commands never have to be remembered or typed correctly. Some of the available commands are **Cut, Copy, Paste** and **Undo,** which can be used to move text and pictures around. These commands are available consistently throughout the system when they are appropriate.

The Smalltalk-76 user interface was a synthesis of three major areas: Alan Kay's models of overlapping windows and the simulation of familiar phenomena, Larry Tesler's work with modeless interfaces, and the evolving Smalltalk language system, built upon the consistent application of a small set of principles. It was implemented on the Alto, itself a synergistic combination of important breakthroughs such as the mouse and the bit-map. As is the case in many syntheses, the whole was greater than the sum of its parts, because the presence of each part strengthened the others. Much of this technology appeared virtually unchanged in the Lisa and Macintosh desktop software, seven years later. Because of the highly iterative nature of the Smalltalk prototype-test-rebuild cycle, it provided an excellent proving ground for a user interface, one which resulted in an extremely effective and well-tuned model.

A Star Is Born

In 1976, a project was begun at Xerox PARC called **Star,** with the intent of producing a powerful bitmapped workstation for commercial release. The hardware was based on the Alto, with a faster processor and more memory. Both Stars and Altos were built around the Xerox-developed local area network, Ethernet. The Star project benefitted heavily from the research-oriented Alto and the Smalltalk community's load of experimental software written for that machine (Reference 6.)

Xerox invested 30 man-years in the user interface design for the Star. Again, the emphasis was upon consistency, transparency, and direct manipulation of objects by pointing. A new dimension, though, was added by the Star team that, although it was based upon previous research, was quite revolutionary. The Star took Alan Kay's concept of simulating everyday experience and created a highly detailed simulation of the environment most familiar to the Star's target audience—the office. Symbols that represented concrete objects, called Icons, were used to convey functions like sending and receiving mail or filing letters. For instance, a small in-basket and out-basket can be pointed to with the mouse to handle electronic mail sent over Ethernet.

These symbols were organized on a grey rectangle, called the **Desktop.** The icons can be moved around on the metaphorical desktop, and arranged as the user sees fit. To select a particular function or to edit a document, the user selects and opens the corresponding icon by pointing with the mouse, and the icon blows up into a window. The goal of the Star design is to have the user directly translate knowledge from his previous experience to the Desktop "world", so that learning time and confusion are reduced to a minimum.

The Star system gave birth to the "desktop metaphor" as we know it today. It was the first commercially viable product from the years of research at LRG, although its $18,000 price tag took it out of the realm of all but the wealthiest businesses. The task of bringing Alan Kay's vision down into the affordably concrete still hadn't been fully met. The Star was released in 1981, close to the time when Alan Kay left Xerox PARC and moved to Atari. The wonderful dream of Dynabook was, unfortunately, still very much a dream.

Lisa

Shortly before Star was released, Larry Tesler also left Xerox and joined the staff at Apple Computer to help design a top-secret new product. He was given the responsibility for over-seeing the applications software on the **Lisa,** which was to be a high-end office system with emphasis upon transparency and ease of use. The Lisa design team drew heavily upon the work done by the Smalltalk group, creating a powerful machine utilizing bitmapped graphics and a one-button mouse, which was thought to be less confusing than the multiple-button versions that had preceded it. Many of the Smalltalk-76 user interface conventions survived on the Lisa intact: modeless interaction, overlapping windows, menus, Cut, Paste and Copy, and the general philosophy of applying a small set of concepts consistently.

To Apple's credit, a good deal of work went into the Lisa interface design to bring it to its present form. Every detail of the interaction between the user and the system was carefully examined, in an attempt to eliminate confusing, "no-win" situations. In the manner of the Star system, the Lisa implementation was governed by a lengthy "user interface standard" document that stated clearly what the position of the designers was on the details of the user's interaction with the system (Reference 7.) The disk drives, for example, were designed not to be removable without the "knowledge and consent"of the systems software. This was done to prevent inadvertent loss of data, which could occur if the diskette were removed while the file system was writing to it.

Lisa brought together the best of the Smalltalk-76 user interface characteristics with the physical metaphor philosophy of the Star, which relied upon icons to communicate functional information to the user instead of using words. Lisa windows are dynamically sizeable by the user, and can be moved to any location on the screen. A standard format for representing windows was established; most windows allow horizontal and vertical scrolling and page advance as well as moving a "thumb" that corresponds to absolute position in the information field.

Lisa Applications

With the introduction of the Lisa, Apple announced seven applications that were integrated into the "office system" desktop environment:

LisaWrite, a word processor; **LisaCalc,** a spreadsheet; **LisaDraw,** a business-oriented drawing package; **LisaGraph,** a graph-generation package; **LisaList,** a list-manager and simple database tool; **LisaProject,** a PERT-oriented project manager, and **LisaTerminal,** which provides VT100-compatible terminal emulation and telecommunications. These all share a common set of principles about how the mouse should be used, how windows should look, and so on, resulting in very low learning time for the entire set of applications. The most severe portion of a new user's learning curve is covered in the first application learned; after that, existing knowledge can be applied to the bulk of the situations encountered in the others. These programs display an unprecedented degree of integration of function in the microcomputer market. Much of this is attributable to the Smalltalk "integrated system" philosophy, in which operating system and applications are virtually indistinguishable (Reference 3.)

Although hailed as a technical success, Lisa was plagued by two problems at its release: somewhat sluggish software and a high price tag. The Lisa announcement price, with bundled applications, was close to $10,000. This was still out of reach for the average manager, who could no doubt benefit greatly from the technology if it were affordable. Consequently, third-party developers were wary of devoting the time necessary to bring up their applications in Lisa's complex development environment, which further isolated the machine. The number of units sold, around 30,000 in 1983, fell far short of internal projections, and many industry observers felt that Lisa's price tag might have severely compromised her (and Apple's) survival in a tough market.

The Appliance Computer

Close to the time that the Lisa project began, Apple also began hatching plans for an "appliance computer" that would be very portable and affordable as well as easy to use. A hardware prototype was implemented using the Motorola 6809 8-bit processor, but was discarded because of inadequate performance. In early 1981, Steve Jobs, the co-founder of Apple, carried his enthusiasm for the dazzling graphics being developed by the Lisa Group over to the engineers working on the new machine. They set to work, creating a 68000-based version of their design, with the goal of achieving 70 percent of Lisa's power at 20 percent of the cost by transporting Lisa's marvelous QuickDraw graphics package, developed by Bill Atkinson. Jobs began taking a personal, emotional interest in the project, and empowered his lieges to raid other departments at Apple and other companies to find the best talent available. The group became a highly motivated, tightly knit unit with a common vision that many felt was a "once in a lifetime" opportunity. The Mac was going to be, in Steve Job's words, "insanely great".

Macintosh

The project, called Macintosh, was the first serious attempt in the history of the personal computer industry to bring the desktop technology in at a mass-market price point. Apple was uniquely qualified to succeed in this venture for several reasons. They had developed the first all-purpose, common denominator, workhorse computer in the Apple II, and organized a company around the goal of bringing computers into the homes, schools and offices of mainstream America. The Lisa I was a costly excursion into the Fortune 500 market that could have been classified as a failure if Apple hadn't learned a lesson from it. They needed to salvage their 200 person-year investment in Lisa software by producing an affordable machine, and in that light, the decision to transport the Lisa graphics package directly to the Macintosh was a brilliant stroke. Finally, the Apple II continued to make Apple cash-rich, and allowed them the luxury of investing $20 million in a highly automated, state-of-the-art production facility capable of generating a million Macs per year.

Clean and Simple

The Macintosh was designed from the ground up to be a mass-producible machine—no hardware options, no slots, and a very low package count on the circuit boards. Heavy use was made of the latest PAL chips, which allow many hardware devices to be condensed into a single package by careful, exacting design work. These factors, together with the large body of expertise available free from the Lisa project, gave the Mac a head start toward success. Apple's targets were the 25 million "knowledge workers" whose jobs involve the manipulation and communication of information. Steve Jobs saw each of them having two "appliances"on their desk: a telephone and a Macintosh.

Another consideration in the Macintosh design was that it occupy a small "footprint", or desk area, and be light enough to carry around between home, school and office. The final package weighs in at 21 pounds and occupies an area only 10 inches square, a refreshing experience after one has tried to make room for an IBM PC on one's desk (or carry it home.) The packaging group utilized a German design firm to help achieve an elegant, pleasing line in the main cabinet and keyboard.

The Macintosh desktop software was necessarily a scaled-down version of that offered by Lisa, since it would only have 128,000 bytes of memory as opposed to Lisa's one million bytes. But the basic conventions involving the mouse, windows, and menus were all maintained, embodying the user interface principles from Smalltalk-76 in yet another context. The principal difference between the Mac and Lisa operating systems lies in the ability to do multi-tasking, a standard feature of the Lisa system, not designed into the Mac because of memory limitations. This difference was relatively transparent to most applications, enabling Apple to develop a migration path for Macintosh software up into the Lisa.

With the Macintosh, Apple announced the Apple 32-bit family, which involved a redesign of the Lisa into three lower-priced, higher performance models that could share software with the Mac. This excellent strategy might well give Lisa the place it deserves in the mainstream corporate world not only by making it affordable, but by inheriting the potentially huge software base that will follow the Macintosh's first year or so of life. The Apple 32-bit family represents an awesome challenge to IBM, DEC, Wang, and other "minicomputer" vendors whose more established office systems may not offer the price/performance value of the Apple line. Traditional distinctions between "minicomputer" and "microcomputer" became suddenly obscured with the onslaught of the low-cost, high-performance 68000 processor; Apple's synthesis of desktop-based software with the 68000 has created a new standard by which personal computing will be judged.

Is Dynabook Here?

Has Alan Kay's vision of the infinite personal tool been achieved? Sadly, not yet. The Macintosh, while bringing bitmapped graphics hardware to a mass audience, is only a beginning step toward Kay's envisioned simulation machine. The Dynabook model described a system in which a powerful yet simple programming and simulation language would be an essential, organic part of the machine, fully integrated with and indistinct from the "operating system". Smalltalk has evolved considerably since 1972, yet remains a somewhat iconoclastic and elite programming environment, one that is large and difficult to implement on small systems. It may be that the "missing link" that would give life to Kay's vision will occur in the near future when the right combination of elegant software and cheap but powerful hardware find each other. If I were to pick candidates for that synthesis today, it would be the Macintosh and some yet-to-be-developed software breakthrough, more efficient and less obscure than anything alive today. You know, that's the most compelling thing about the Macintosh. It does start you thinking about doing the impossible!

References

1. Kay, A. "Microelectronics and the Personal Computer." Scientific American, September, 1977.
2. English, W, D Englebart, and M Berman, "Display-Selection Techniques for Text Manipulation." IEEE Transactions on Human Factors in Electronics, Volume 8, Number 1, pages 21 through 31, 1977.
3. Tesler, L "The Smalltalk Environment." BYTE, August, 1981.
4. Nelson, T. Computer Lib/Dream Machines. South Bend, IN. The Distributors: 1974.
5. Wadlow, T "The Xerox Alto Computer." BYTE, September, 1981.
6. Smith, D, C. Irby, R. Kimball, B. Verplank and E Harslem. "Designing the Star User Interface." BYTE, April, 1982.
7. Morgan, C, G. Williams, and P. Lemmons, "An Interview with Wayne Rosing, Bruce Daniels, and Larry Tesler." BYTE , February, 1983.
8. Williams, G. "The Apple Macintosh Computer." BYTE, February, 1984.
9. Lemmons, P. "An Interview: The Macintosh Design Team." BYTE, February, 1984.
10. Kay, A, A. Goldberg, "Personal Dynamic Media." Computer, March, 1977.

B

Macintosh Versus IBM PC: A Comparison

Unfair But Necessary

This chapter is by its very nature an unfair enterprise. The PC has been out for several years, and consequently has an established software base; the Macintosh, on the other hand, has had the benefit of newer technology such as the Sony drives. But because this comparison will be on the mind of nearly every shopper who considers buying a Macintosh or a PC, it must be attempted, unfair or not. The Macintosh has inevitably been cast into the role of the brash young challenger attempting to unseat the world champion, and their title match cannot be ignored.

While this chapter is unfair, it is also subjective, and can only be based upon the experience of its author. I have been and will continue to be a software developer on both machines, so my opinions are based on long hours of work as a programmer, writer and user of the various applications on the PC and the Mac. The opinions expressed herein are mine alone.

Processor

There is no contest in this round, because the 8088 is an 8/16 bit processor against the 68000, a 16/32 bit chip with a faster basic cycle time and more powerful instruction set. Our benchmarks in chapter 18 probably reflected this disparity in CPU power more than anything else. Because the Macintosh has a much more complex Operating System, common user operations will often be similar in speed. The difference will be seen most clearly inside applications when very computation-intensive operations occur, such as updating spreadsheet cells.

Decision:
Mac wins this one on newer technology.

Memory

The PC has a theoretical maximum of 640 Kilobytes. Because many applications currently running on the PC were converted from 8-bit environments, memory space over 64 or 128K is often not supported. Also, vendors hesitate to require the full complement of RAM because there is such a wide variety of hardware configurations in the PC, and the least common denominator is the safest configuration to support. The 8088 and 8086, because of their segmented architecture, make handling over 64K a rather tricky task for the programmer. Therefore, if the extra memory is present, it often gets used for RAM disk simulation, which speeds certain things up, but is dangerous from the point of view of data security because everything is lost if power goes.

The Mac had 128K at its introduction, but will almost certainly be expanded to 512K when 256K-bit memory chips become widely available. The advantage then will be that developers can safely exploit the full 512K without worrying about cutting out part of their user base, so applications will be able to truly exploit the full memory space. An additional memory advantage is gained because of the 64K ROM in the Macintosh, which holds code that would require much more space if implemented within an application. Emulation of the 64K Macintosh ROM would easily take 128K or more on an 8088-based machine.

Decision:
The PC over the 128K Mac. A slight edge to the 512K Mac because of its standardized configuration and non-segmented architecture.

Video Display

IBM's monochrome display, while it has excellent clarity, is crippled in that it doesn't support graphics. The graphics adapter card from IBM provides poor quality in text mode. It is burdened by glitching and has only black and white available in high-resolution mode (640 by 200 dots.)

The Macintosh has a 512 by 342 dot display that provides excellent clarity because of its high bandwidth monitor. While color is not a part of the Mac's current design, the QuickDraw graphics support code has all of the hooks necessary to support color if and when high-resolution color displays become cheap enough to be practical in a future Macintosh model.

Decision:
The Macintosh is the winner because of its high-quality black and white graphics and non-glitching display circuitry.

Disks

The PC has 320K 5¼″ double-sided double-density floppy disks. The drives are fairly reliable, and the MS/DOS file system is efficient.

The Mac's 3½″ disks are a distinct pleasure to use because they're small, tough and easy to store and transport. The Mac uses single-sided 400K drives until double-sided 800K drives become available. Until then, 400K just isn't enough. The Finder and its cousins eat up over half the disk, so room for data is dear on the single-sided drives. Fortunately, the sophistication of the Finder makes having one drive livable instead of intolerable, but most people will probably opt for the second drive,as most do with the PC.

Decision:
The PC over the 400K Mac, but when 800K drives come in, look out, PC. On the basis of media alone, the Sonys win.

Sound Generation

The PC's sound section is an exercise in parsimony. A simple clock chip that can be programmed to generate a square wave of any frequency is tied through a driver to a speaker. This configuration is easy to use for simple things, but cannot support multiple voices or other waveforms than square wave. Also, a lot of tricky applications support is needed to play sounds while the program is doing other things.

The Mac's four-voice sound synthesis capability is one of the most sophisticated in the field, but requires a good deal of software support. It has a square-wave mode that's as easy to use as the PC's. When fully exploited, this part of the Mac will be truly spectacular.

Decision:
The Macintosh is clearly the winner in this area.

Keyboards

Rarely were so many people so upset as when IBM released its personal computer with a keyboard that had the shift and carriage return keys in the wrong place for touch-typists (excepting perhaps when IBM released its toy-like keyboard on the PC/Jr.) "Wrong" in this case means that IBM violated its own standard, set with the Selectric typewriter. Other than that grave error, the PC keyboard is unequalled in its feel and quality.

Ironically, the Mac and Lisa keyboards obey the Selectric legend more faithfully than does the PC. Touch typists will have no trouble with either one, because they're identical. In terms of feel, the Mac is good, but the PC is excellent. The Mac's keyboard is much simpler because of the burden taken from it by the mouse.

Decision:
The Mac wins because of its ease of use for touch typists and novices, who are overwhelmed by all of the keys on the PC. You still can't beat the PC keyboard for touch and solid quality.

Expansion Hardware

The PC is an open-architecture machine, meaning that IBM published the details of its hardware implementation for the world to see and (copy.) It has 5 slots, of which one is used for the display card, one for the disk controller, and a third if communications or more memory is needed. A huge market for add-on cards that did everything under the sun arose instantly for the PC, but this introduced a compatibility problem for software writers, because you can never be sure exactly what's in the PC's slots.

The Mac was built with no internal expansion possible. It includes, however, more hardware capability than the typical PC with three slots filled. Also, a "virtual slot" scheme has been developed for the Mac's RS-422 ports that enables smart external devices to function as though they were installed in the Mac's main cabinet. The payoff is that a software author knows that every Mac comes off the assembly line with the same very capable hardware configuration, and can safely exploit all of it. The implications for ease of assembly are enormous.

> **Decision:**
> The Mac, because it provides expandability with all of the advantages of a standardized basic configuration that is truly functional.

Communications

The PC enjoys a favored position among many corporate DP managers simply because it has their three favorite initials stamped on the front. They know where to look when they want to tie all of those new PCs in as workstations on the big IBM mainframe. By now, the PC has communicated with virtually every other IBM machine that is still used. This has much less to do with technical excellence than with its surname.

Apple has taken a bold step in the communications arena by adopting RS-422 as the standard for its Apple 32 family. This represents a commitment to the future while it maintains compatibility with current RS-232 standards. Apple has also gone after the corporate mainframe environment with its cluster controller and 3278 emulation, but will remain hampered by an imbedded IBM consciousness in that world. The AppleBus peripheral-sharing scheme promises to create a suitable basis for genuine LAN technology at a later time.

> **Decision:**
> The Macintosh, for its innovation and Apple's aggressive pursuit of communications excellence for the Apple 32 line.

Packaging

The IBM PC, because it received far less effort toward optimization of package count than the Mac, is large and heavy. The entire Macintosh has less chips than the video card alone in the PC. Carrying a PC is not a task that anyone would want to repeat. Its "footprint" is over 450 inches, which eats up a lot of desk. Some may appreciate the fact that the PC is big and heavy, because it gives them a sense of security.

The Macintosh occupies around 200 inches of desk area. Its package, created by a German design firm, tends toward the vertical, making it easy to carry. The enclosure has an integral handle molded into the top, and weighs a little over 20 pounds with keyboard. The MacPack carrying case is designed for transporting the Mac from home to office or classroom, and is quite functional.

Decision:
The Mac for the finest packaging in the personal computer industry to date.

Operating Systems

MS/DOS represented a vast improvement over CP/M in its time with respect to ease of use, but still demands that the user memorize many commands and function keys to use it effectively. It is fairly small considering its function. MS/DOS 2.0 and 2.1 improve the I/O methodology, making it device independent in the manner of UNIX. The PC BIOS, which enables MS/DOS to work with the PC hardware, is well documented and clearly written. Very little support is provided for the graphics and sound devices, this being left to the application or its language environment.

The Macintosh Finder inherited a lot of its approach from the Lisa Office System, a well-planned user interface (see Appendix A.) The Finder in its first release possessed some annoying characteristics related to copying with single-drive systems, and program loading was rather slow. Nevertheless, the Finder removes the barrier between the user and the machine, and effectively disappears as an Operating System. This would seem to be the goal of any systems designer, because Operating Systems are not a natural or comfortable concept for novice users to grasp. The Finder is useful for novices and experts alike, in contrast to such questionable experiments as Valdocs™. The level of systems support in the Macintosh User Interface Toolbox for graphics and the interface in general is unparalleled in the industry.

Decision:
The Macintosh, although the Finder needs some attention to rough edges.

Software Design Philosophy

IBM has no clear-cut design philosophy with respect to PC applications, other than a suggestion in the back of some manuals that designers use certain keys for certain things, which many vendors seem to have ignored. Even within IBM Logo products, there are no conventions as to user interface, which means that you have to start at ground zero in learning any new application. Although several much-heralded window-based environments are being developed for the PC, they seem to share no conventions. Microsoft has decided to support the Macintosh standard in their Windows product for the PC, but its release date is uncertain. A new level of irony would be reached if the PC became thought of as a "Macintosh compatible."

Apple's promotion of the Macintosh User Interface Guidelines would have failed had they not been effective and well-designed. Undoubtedly, there will be vendors that ignore this standard, but it appears that the majority will accept it, because of its indisputable benefits. A user can learn a new application in minutes instead of hours if they understand how to use the control structure of the program before they start. The standard owes its quality to years of accumulated research in Smalltalk and the Lisa (see Appendix A.)

Decision:
The Mac by default.

Developer Support

IBM seems to pride itself on maintaining a cool to nonexistent relationship with software developers. Many developers have found infinite frustration in attempting to wade through the massive Big Blue Bureaucracy in hopes of getting their products looked at. Fortunately, IBM has made it a point to publish excellent technical information on their products, eliminating the need to deal directly with IBM's maze of technical support offices.

Apple has set up an excellent program in which developers can become Certified, and therefore be eligible for direct support on product hardware and software. Dealers are generally well-trained, and hotlines are maintained for technical support on all Apple products. Close pre-release developer relations on both the Mac and IIc projects have resulted in high-quality software being available soon after the release of the product, which aids the consumer as well as Apple. It could be a sign of the times that Microsoft's Chairman, Bill Gates, has publicly compared the Mac favorably against the PC, and stated that the Mac should account for over 50% of Microsoft's 1984 revenues.

Decision:
Macintosh.

Service

Both companies pride themselves on well-established, well-trained service networks. Because the Mac is a closed box from the point of view of the user, less is likely to go wrong with it as a result of incorrectly installed boards and the like. The low package count of the Mac could well make it a more reliable machine than the PC, but the jury will remain out until a track record has been established.

Decision:
A tie; too close to call until more information is in.

Product availability

The IBM PC stunned the personal computer industry with the avalanche of third-party products that appeared within a year of its release. Initial concern that the PC wasn't CP/M compatible became irrelevant as everything was converted to run on the PC anyway. Part of this can be attributed to the relative ease of converting Z-80 and 8080 code to run on the 8088. Because of the PC's open architecture, the third-party hardware market exploded as quickly as software, spawning a number of imitators that further embedded the PC as a standard.

It is highly unlikely that the Macintosh will be able to compete with the PC in terms of sheer quantity of available products. Because it is a more powerful and complex machine internally, developing for the Mac is a major resource commitment, not to be taken lightly. It will probably take a year for developers to get over the worst part of the learning curve and become really productive with the User Interface Toolbox. Enough developer interest has been registered for a critical mass to develop that will result in an explosion of products, but this will occur neither as quickly or with such force as that seen with the PC.

On the other side of the coin, a weeding-out process will reduce the number of quick, poorly planned conversions and imitations of other products, and result in a higher overall quality for the entire group. Apple will provide design advice if requested, which will encourage adherence to the User Interface Guidelines. From what we've already seen, it seems likely that the user will have as many top products to choose from, and a lot less trash.

Decision:
The PC is a clear winner in terms of quality, but this could eventually be offset by the high standards being set for Macintosh products.

Documentation

IBM's manuals for the PC tend to be voluminous, complete, and not terribly clear. They are definitely not written for novices, and are poor for reference because of erratic indexing and organization. Their sheer size can produce anxiety in new users.

Apple set new standards for user documentation with its series of manuals for the Lisa. The Macintosh has exceeded those standards, and is easily the most attractive and useful set of user documents in the industry. The written documentation is supported by clever and attractive "Guided Tour" demonstration disks and audio tapes for those who would rather not dive into manuals right away.

Decision:
Macintosh for advancing the documentation state of the art.

Price

It is difficult to create a fair price comparison between these two machines because they are so different. For instance, how much RAM would the Macintosh ROM be worth in the PC? Treat this comparison as a ballpark estimate based upon some educated guesses. Other analysts will have

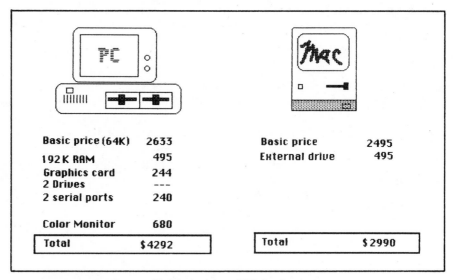

Figure B.1   Prices for Comparable Macintosh and PC Configurations.

other opinions, and you should take all of them into consideration before making a purchase. Figure B-1 summarizes 1984 prices for what I consider to be a reasonably comparable hardware configuration of each machine.

Decision:
The Mac easily wins the price/performance breakdown. While it is unlikely, we could see a change in IBM's pricing policy for the PC.

Overall score

For the 128K Mac with 400K drives, the Macintosh 12, the PC 3 and 1 tie. For the 512K Mac with 800K drives, the Macintosh 14, the PC 1 and 1 tie.

Glossary

Action Buttons: In dialog boxes, a form of control that causes a system action when selected with the mouse.

Address Bus: The electrical lines in a computer that carry the address currently being operated on by the CPU.

Alert Box: A Dialog that is intended to make you aware of an unusual condition.

Amplitude: The amount of magnitude variation in some measurable phenomenon, such as sound, from its zero level.

ANSI: The American National Standards Institute.

Application: A program on the Macintosh that is started up by the Finder in response to a user's choice. An application is a tool that helps the user perform a useful task, such as drawing or writing.

Ascii Codes: A set of numeric codes assigned to the symbols that are displayable in text on computers and printers.

Assembly Language: The set of instructions that a CPU can understand directly. Assembly language is a symbolic representation for machine language, which is composed of numbers that are commands to the CPU.

Asynchronous: A mode of communications in which character transmissions are not tied to a clock, but are sent as they become available. Start and stop bits are used to synchronize the two computers before and after each character.

Balanced Lines: An electrical configuration in which two lines contain the same signal, but of opposite polarity. Noise, which is common on both lines, then can be detected and canceled out by the receiver.

Bandwidth: The range of frequencies that a device can respond to and still remain within specified performance values. Higher-bandwidth devices are usually more expensive.

Baud: Bits per second; used to express communications speeds. Bell 212 A: The most common 1200-baud modem protocol for dialup use in North America.

Benchmark Programs: Short programs used to demonstrate speed differences between various computers or languages.

Binary Arithmetic: Arithmetic done in base 2, in which the only digit values are 0 and 1.

Bit: The basic unit of information in digital computers; derived as a shortened form of BInary digiT. A bit can have a value of either 0 or 1.

Bitmap: A display technique utilizing an area of memory to hold the dot values for the screen. A bit is used for each dot on the screen.

Block: A region of the disk, the basic unit of allocation in the file system. A block in the Macintosh is 512 bytes.

Boilerplate: Text that is re-used frequently, such as a standard paragraph in a contract.

Boot Blocks: The first two blocks on a Macintosh disk, read when the system starts up, or boots, from the disk.

Buffer: A region of memory that is used to hold data so it can be manipulated by software.

Byte: Eight bits, which is enough to hold an Ascii value for one character.

Call: To transfer control to another software module so that it can perform calculations or I/O and return with a result.

Cell: In spreadsheet applications, the basic unit of information that is the intersection of a column and a row. Cells can generally hold text, numbers or formulas.

Character: A single text symbol. Characters each require one byte of storage.

Character Generator: A hardware device that has bit patterns for all of the Ascii codes stored in its internal ROM. When passed a character value, the character generator sends the correct bit pattern to the video section for display of that character.

Check Boxes: Controls, seen in dialogs, that can be on (checked) or off.

Chip: An integrated circuit, which is a silicon wafer etched in a manner that generates hundreds or thousands of transistors and other devices in a very small area. The silicon chip is placed in a plastic carrier for protection and convenience.

Clear to Send: One of the RS-232 signals that is used to establish a "handshake", or synchronized connection, between two ends of a communications link.

Click: To depress the mouse button and release it rapidly.

Clipboard: A holding area for data that has been Cut or Copied using the Edit menu. This is the means by which data can be moved between applications.

Clipping: Not displaying the portion of a figure that is hidden by a window boundary or another figure, providing an illusion of depth.

Close Box: A small rectangle in the upper left corner of many windows that results in the window disappearing when it is selected with the mouse.

Code: The statements in a program that command the computer to perform certain functions under specified conditions.

Command Key: The key with the cloverleaf symbol that is used on the Macintosh as a "shortcut" key. When pressed in combination with an appropriate key, it can cause the selection of a menu option as if the mouse had been used.

Command: An action selectable on a menu or by using the Command key.

Communications: The process of exchanging data between two computers or a computer and a terminal.

Compiler: A program that translates statements written in a high-level language such as Pascal into machine language.

Controls: Buttons, dials, check boxes and other means by which a user can control an application's parameters within a dialog or a window.

Coordinate system: A mapping that assigns locations to points; a grid.

Copy: To duplicate a selection from a document into the Clipboard, replacing whatever was there previously.

CPU: The Central Processing Unit; the programmable device that controls the other devices in a computer and provides most of its power.

CRT: A Cathode-ray tube. A display device that works by illuminating a phosphor-coated screen with electrons projected from a heated element.

Cursor: The pointer that moves with the mouse; often has an arrow shape.

Cut: To remove a selection from a document, placing it in the Clipboard.

Cycle: One complete occurence of a repetitive phenomenon.

Data: The information stored and manipulated by a computer, stored as a sequence of on/off states known as bits.

Data Base: An organized assemblage of data into logical units; the program used to manage data organized in this manner.

Debug: To run a program, observing its behavior in an effort to flush out any problems that might occur.

Desk Accessories: Several miniature applications that can run simultaneously with a normal application, providing useful functions such as a clock and Notepad.

Desktop: The gray area of the Macintosh screen, together with the menu bar at the top.

Dials: Continuously variable controls, such as the elevator box in a scroll bar.

Digital: Refers to anything that encodes information as binary digits, or bits.

Direct Memory Access (DMA): The process in which a secondary device takes over the address bus for a short time and uses the computer's memory instead of requesting the information from the CPU.

Directory: A listing of all of the files on a given disk volume.

Disk Controller: The hardware device that sends control signals to the disk drive and moves the heads to their proper positions.

Document: A collection of information that can be manipulated by a certain application.

DOS: A Disk Operating System.

Double-click: To depress the mouse button rapidly in succession.

Download: To transfer data from one computer to another via a communications link.

Drag: To hold down the mouse button while moving the mouse.

Edit: On the Macintosh, the standard editing commands are Cut, Copy and Paste. In general, modifying the appearance of text or pictures.

EIA: The Electronic Industries Association.

Eject: To release the disk from its locked position in the drive, so that it can be removed.

Extensible: Any language that can have its essential characteristics modified so that it behaves like a different language is considered extensible. Forth, Smalltalk and Lisp are extensible languages.

File: A named collection of data.

Finder: The program that starts up when the Macintosh is turned on, and creates the desktop and its functioning.

Font: A set of characters with common size and stylistic characteristics.

Forth: A language, developed by Charles Moore, that has many attractive properties for personal computing, including speed and space efficiency; sometimes called more of an art than a science.

Glitching: The tendency of some video displays to show snow or ragged lines when certain computation is performed. The Macintosh is completely immune from glitching.

GrafPort: A data structure that supplies parameters for QuickDraw, creating a self-contained drawing environment. Each window has its own GrafPort.

Heads: The parts of a tape deck or disk drive that magnetically encode and read information to and from magnetic media.

Heap: The section of memory which holds variable-length data that can come and go dynamically.

Host: A large central computer used to support dialup communications from many smaller machines.

Hot Spot: The point on the cursor that is considered its exact location, such as the tip of the arrow.

I/O: Input/Output; that part of a computer that deals with the outside world.

Icon: A symbolic representation of a tangible object, such as a trashcan.

Interface: The point of connection between two separate systems, at which some form of communication can occur.

Interpreter: A language processor that translates language statements as they are entered, providing a friendlier, less constrained environment than a compiler.

Interrupt Handler: A small segment of program code that is entered when the processor must respond quickly to some event, such as a key being typed.

Justification: Aligning both sides of a body of text by inserting spaces between words. Performed automatically by many word processors.

Kilobyte (K): 1024 bytes; a basic unit of measure for both disk and memory space, convenient in computer use because it is a power of two.

Linker: A program that can combine separately compiled modules into to a single executable program.

Local Area Network: A means of connecting several small computers together so that they can exchange information without having to physically copy disks or tapes.

Mainframe: A large computer, often costing millions of dollars.

Megabyte (Mb): One million bytes.

Memory: The part of a computer that can retain information and make it available at a later time.

Menu: A box that allows the selection of a command by pointing with the mouse.

Menu Bar: The horizontal bar across the top of the Macintosh screen with names of menus inside it.

Mode: An artificial constraint imposed upon a user by the designer of an application in which common actions might have unfamiliar meanings.

Modem: A device that translates digital data into sound so that it can be transmitted and received via telephone lines.

Mouse: A device that can be used to guide a pointer around on the screen by rolling the mouse on a flat surface. Mice also have from one to three buttons to generate command information.

Open: The process of selecting a file or icon for use.

Operating System: The software that manages the various hardware devices in a system so that an application can deal with them using relatively simple calls.

Option Key: A key to the left of the command key, used to generate the graphics character set and as an analog for what some systems consider the "Control" key.

Pane: A division of a window into a number of rectangular regions.

Parallel: Occurring simultaneously; a parallel port is one in which all 8 data bits are sent together rather than in sequence.

Parameter RAM: A small region of the Macintosh memory that retains its information when power is off. It is used to store the current time as well as convenience settings altered from the Control Panel Desk Accessory.

Parity: A method of using an extra data bit for each byte as an error detection scheme in character transmission or memory; parity provides a counter-check to help detect a malfunction.

Paste: To copy the contents of the Clipboard, inserting it in the current document.

Pattern: An 8 by 8 matrix of dots that is repeated to form patterns in QuickDraw. This technique is used to generate the gray desktop and patterns in MacPaint.

Peripheral: An external hardware device, such as a printer or disk.

Pointer: The graphical entity that moves in response to mouse motion.

Port: A device that the CPU can use for communication with the external world.

Primitive: A fundamental object or operation that can be used to build more complex structures.

Protocol: An agreed-upon method for I/O operations, in which a specified series of steps is performed in a predetermined sequence.

Queue: A buffer that holds elements in the order that they were added. The first element added is the the first to be removed.

QuickDraw: The graphics software that provides the foundation for the entire Macintosh user interface as well as the MacPaint application.

Radio Buttons: Controls that can only be selected one at a time; if one button is selected, the others turn off.

RAM: Random-Access Memory. Unless battery backup is provided, RAM loses its contents when power to the machine is removed.

Region: An arbitrary area of a drawing in QuickDraw.

Register: A very fast holding area for data. Microprocessor registers are from 8 to 32 bits wide.

Resolution: The number of horizontal and vertical dots in a video display; alternately, the number of dots per inch.

Resource: Anything related to screen display, such as window formats, menu formats, text strings, etc., can be built as resources, which are separate from the program code and easier to change. This allows an English-language application to be converted to French without a major revision of the code.

Rollover: The number of keys that a keyboard can detect without error when pressed simultaneously.

ROM: Read-Only Memory. ROM cannot be modified, and retains its contents when power is off.

RS-232C: An electrical standard for communications that uses unbalanced lines. Line lengths are usually limited to 50-100 feet, and speeds to under 19,200 baud.

RS-422: An electrical standard for communications that uses balanced lines. Runs of several thousand feet and much higher speeds are possible with this standard than with the older RS-232C.

SDLC: Synchronous Data Link Control; A communications protocol developed by IBM that allows a master station to simultaneously send to one remote station while receiving from another. Each station is assigned a unique Station Address for identification.

Sector: The basic unit of organization on disks. A sector consists of a data area and a control area that is used by the file system.

Select: To point to a graphical object and click the mouse button. The selected object is highlighted on the display.

Serial: To process sequentially rather than simultaneously.

Software: The instructions written by programmers that cause computer hardware to behave in a useful way.

Spreadsheet: A file that contains rows and columns, each of which contains on of several types of data (see Cell.) Spreadsheets are useful for financial planning, because they permit instant feedback of results as parameters are changed.

Stack: A buffer that maintains elements in order. The last element added is the first to be removed.

String: A sequence of text characters.

Synchronous: A mode of communications in which characters must be sent at regularly occurring intervals marked by a clock pulse. Synchronous communications is generally faster than asynchronous because of improved error detection.

Terminal: A device used for communicationg with a computer that provides a serial interface, keyboard and display, but is not capable of computation in its own right.

Text: Readable characters, each of which is encoded as 1 byte.

Throughput: A measure of the total workload capacity of a device, such as a CPU or I/O chip.

Tiling: A method of arranging overlapping windows that allows easy access to any window.

Timbre: The quality of a sound, such as the mellowness of a flute or the piercing sharpness of a trumpet. Timbre is unrelated to the frequency, or pitch or a sound.

Toolbox: The collection of system code in the Macintosh ROM that provides the components of the desktop, including windows, menus, dialogs, and so on.

Track: A curcular band around a disk that contains a number of sectors. Macintosh disks have 80 tracks on each side.

Trap: An instruction that interrupts the CPU and tells it to jump to a special piece of system code, and then return.

Undo: A command that allows a user to reverse the consequences of the last action. This is very valuable for new users, because it permits experimentation without fear.

User Interface: The software in an application or operating system that manages the exchange of information with the user, including the keyboard, mouse and display. This is one of the most complex and least understood areas of software design.

User Interface Guidelines: A document published by Apple for developers that specifies a common method of handling the mouse, menus, dialogs, and so on. It is aimed at encouraging a consistency in applications that will greatly benefit the user.

Variable: A named storage location in memory that can be read from or written to by using its name.

Volume: A method of organizing files into a common named storage area. Macintosh floppy disks have a single volume, while hard disks can each have several volumes assigned to them.

Waveform: A graph representing the variation in amplitude in a sound over time, generally for a single cycle of the wave.

Window: A named, rectangular division of the screen that can be moved and sized according to the user's wishes.

Word Processor: An application that permits the entry, editing and formatting of text for presentation.

Index